MASTERPEACE MANDALAS

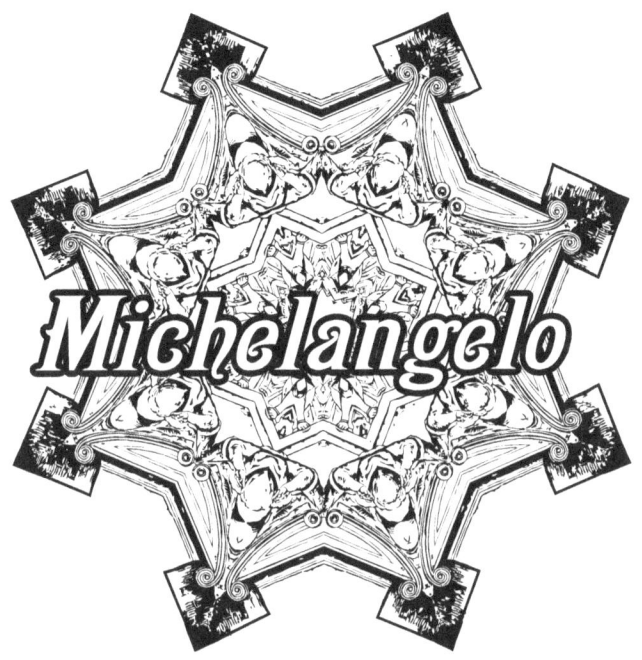

MICHELANGELO
Coloring Book
VOLUME 1

This book does not recommend, promote or advise any diagnosis
or treatment for any condition and is not a substitute
for qualified professional consultation. But it could be fun.

Michelangelo Masterpeace Mandalas Coloring Book Volume 1

ISBN-10: 194438104X
ISBN-13: 978-1-944381-04-2

stop by and tell us what you think
www.masterpeacebooks.com

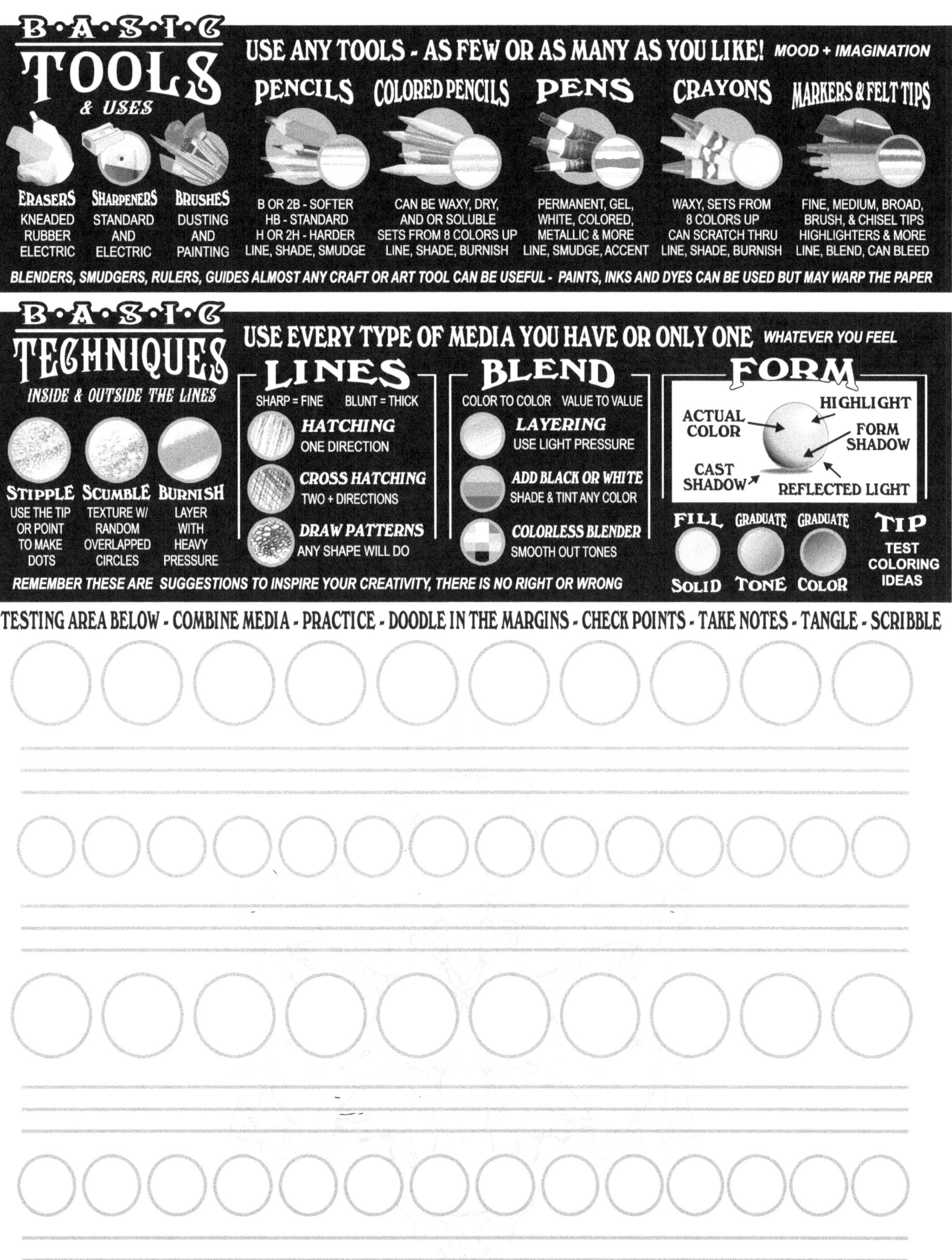

B·A·S·I·C TOOLS & USES

USE ANY TOOLS - AS FEW OR AS MANY AS YOU LIKE! *MOOD + IMAGINATION*

ERASERS
KNEADED
RUBBER
ELECTRIC

SHARPENERS
STANDARD
AND
ELECTRIC

BRUSHES
DUSTING
AND
PAINTING

PENCILS
B OR 2B - SOFTER
HB - STANDARD
H OR 2H - HARDER
LINE, SHADE, SMUDGE

COLORED PENCILS
CAN BE WAXY, DRY,
AND OR SOLUBLE
SETS FROM 8 COLORS UP
LINE, SHADE, BURNISH

PENS
PERMANENT, GEL,
WHITE, COLORED,
METALLIC & MORE
LINE, SMUDGE, ACCENT

CRAYONS
WAXY, SETS FROM
8 COLORS UP
CAN SCRATCH THRU
LINE, SHADE, BURNISH

MARKERS & FELT TIPS
FINE, MEDIUM, BROAD,
BRUSH, & CHISEL TIPS
HIGHLIGHTERS & MORE
LINE, BLEND, CAN BLEED

BLENDERS, SMUDGERS, RULERS, GUIDES ALMOST ANY CRAFT OR ART TOOL CAN BE USEFUL - PAINTS, INKS AND DYES CAN BE USED BUT MAY WARP THE PAPER

B·A·S·I·C TECHNIQUES
INSIDE & OUTSIDE THE LINES

USE EVERY TYPE OF MEDIA YOU HAVE OR ONLY ONE *WHATEVER YOU FEEL*

STIPPLE
USE THE TIP
OR POINT
TO MAKE
DOTS

SCUMBLE
TEXTURE W/
RANDOM
OVERLAPPED
CIRCLES

BURNISH
LAYER
WITH
HEAVY
PRESSURE

LINES
SHARP = FINE   BLUNT = THICK

HATCHING
ONE DIRECTION

CROSS HATCHING
TWO + DIRECTIONS

DRAW PATTERNS
ANY SHAPE WILL DO

BLEND
COLOR TO COLOR   VALUE TO VALUE

LAYERING
USE LIGHT PRESSURE

ADD BLACK OR WHITE
SHADE & TINT ANY COLOR

COLORLESS BLENDER
SMOOTH OUT TONES

FORM
HIGHLIGHT
ACTUAL COLOR
FORM SHADOW
CAST SHADOW
REFLECTED LIGHT

FILL SOLID   **GRADUATE** TONE   **GRADUATE** COLOR

TIP
TEST
COLORING
IDEAS

REMEMBER THESE ARE SUGGESTIONS TO INSPIRE YOUR CREATIVITY, THERE IS NO RIGHT OR WRONG

TESTING AREA BELOW - COMBINE MEDIA - PRACTICE - DOODLE IN THE MARGINS - CHECK POINTS - TAKE NOTES - TANGLE - SCRIBBLE

Tip - Carefully Remove The Last Page Of This Book And Place It Under The Page Your Working On To Protect The Next Page
REMEMBER THERE IS NO RIGHT OR WRONG WAY TO COLOR - COLOR HOW YOU FEEL - WHEN YOU FEEL - AND AS LONG AS YOU FEEL

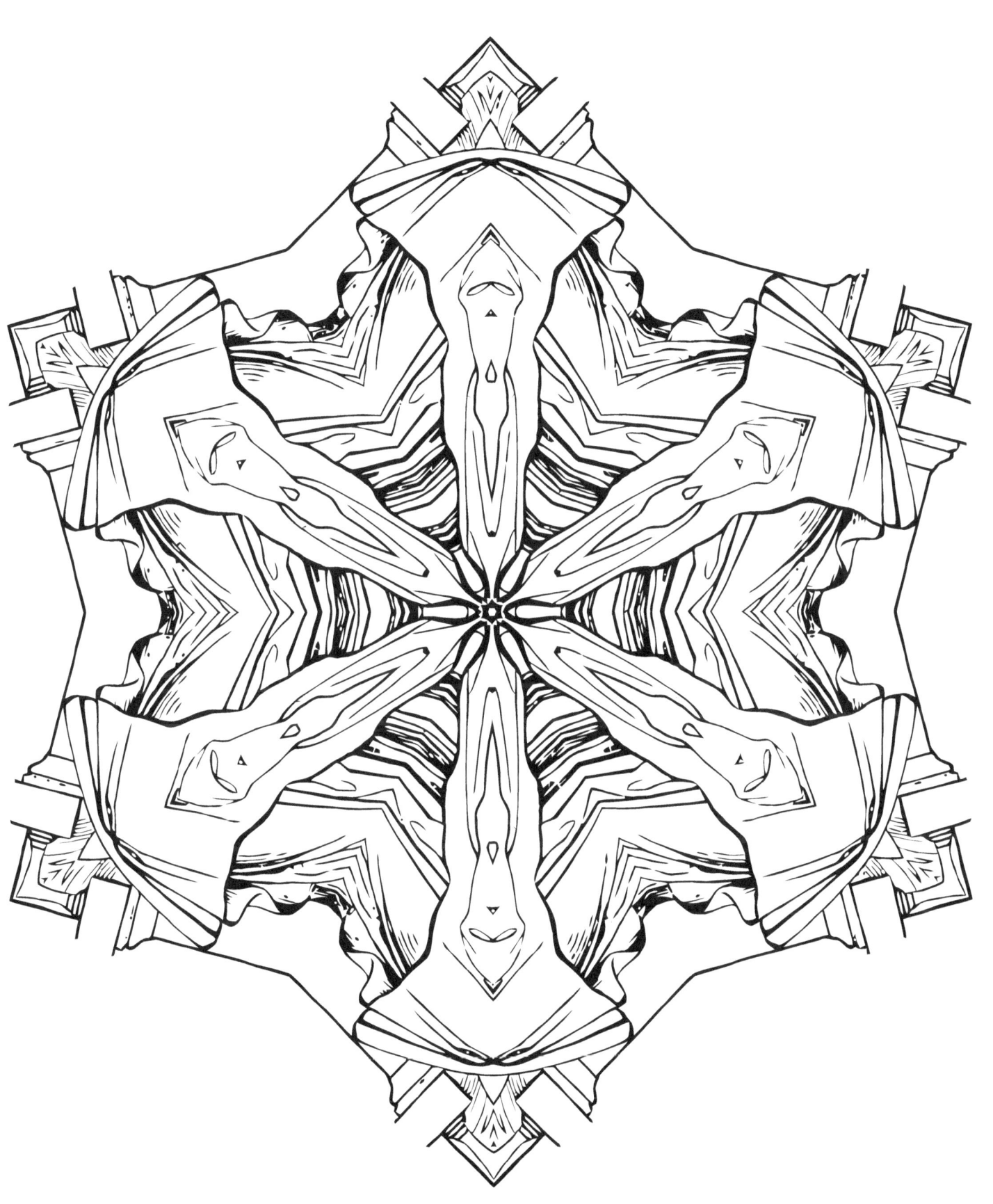

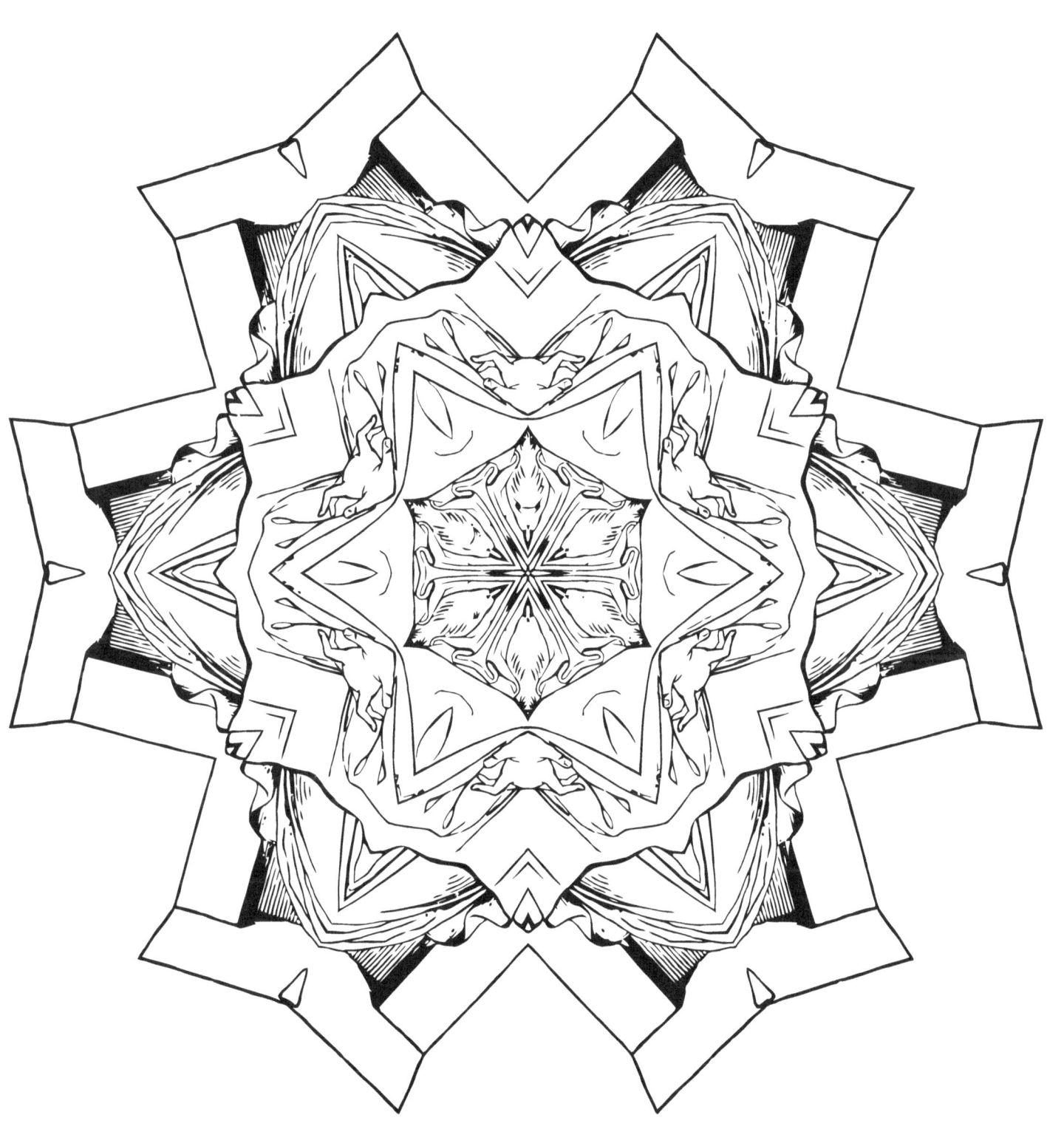

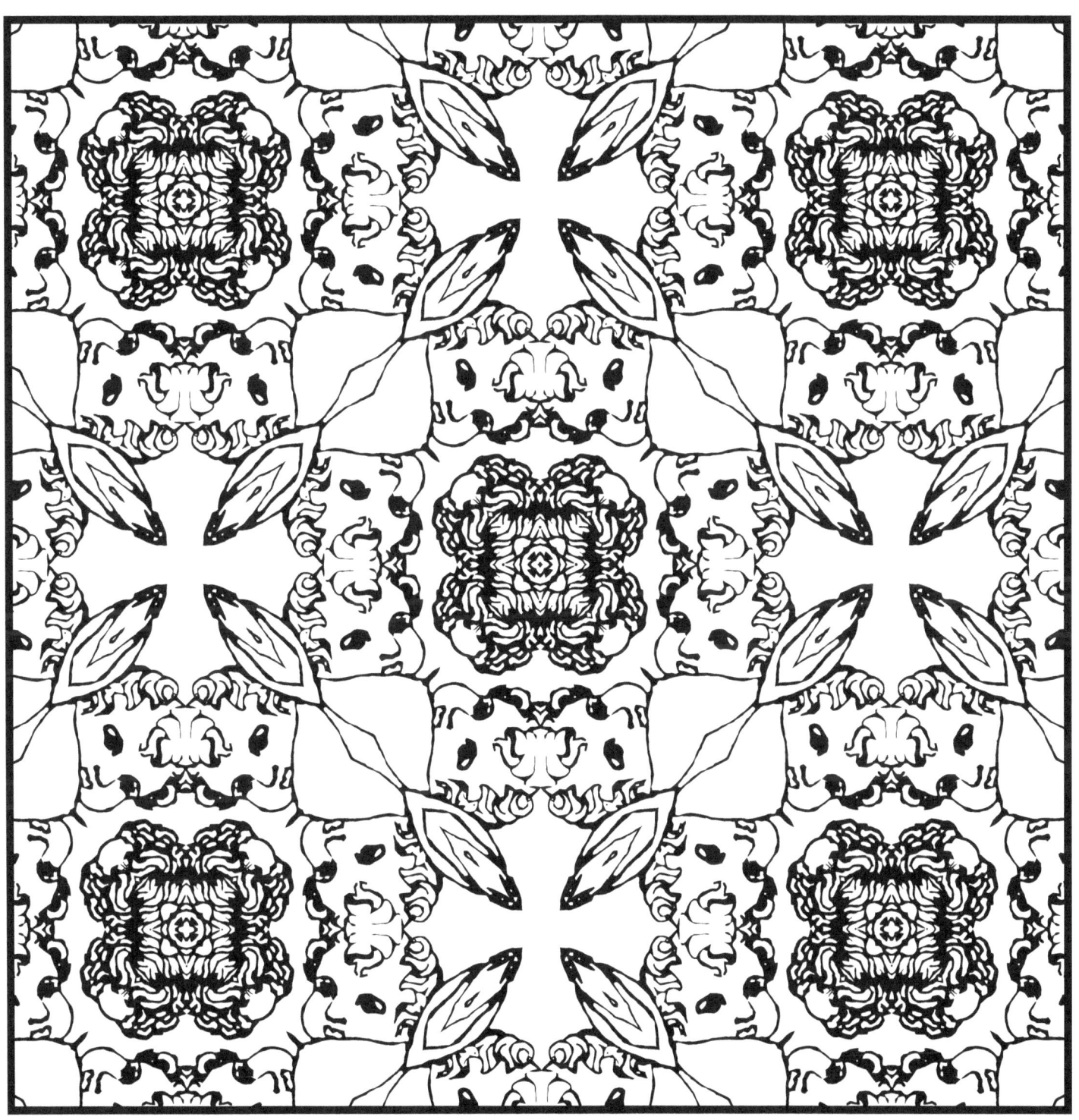

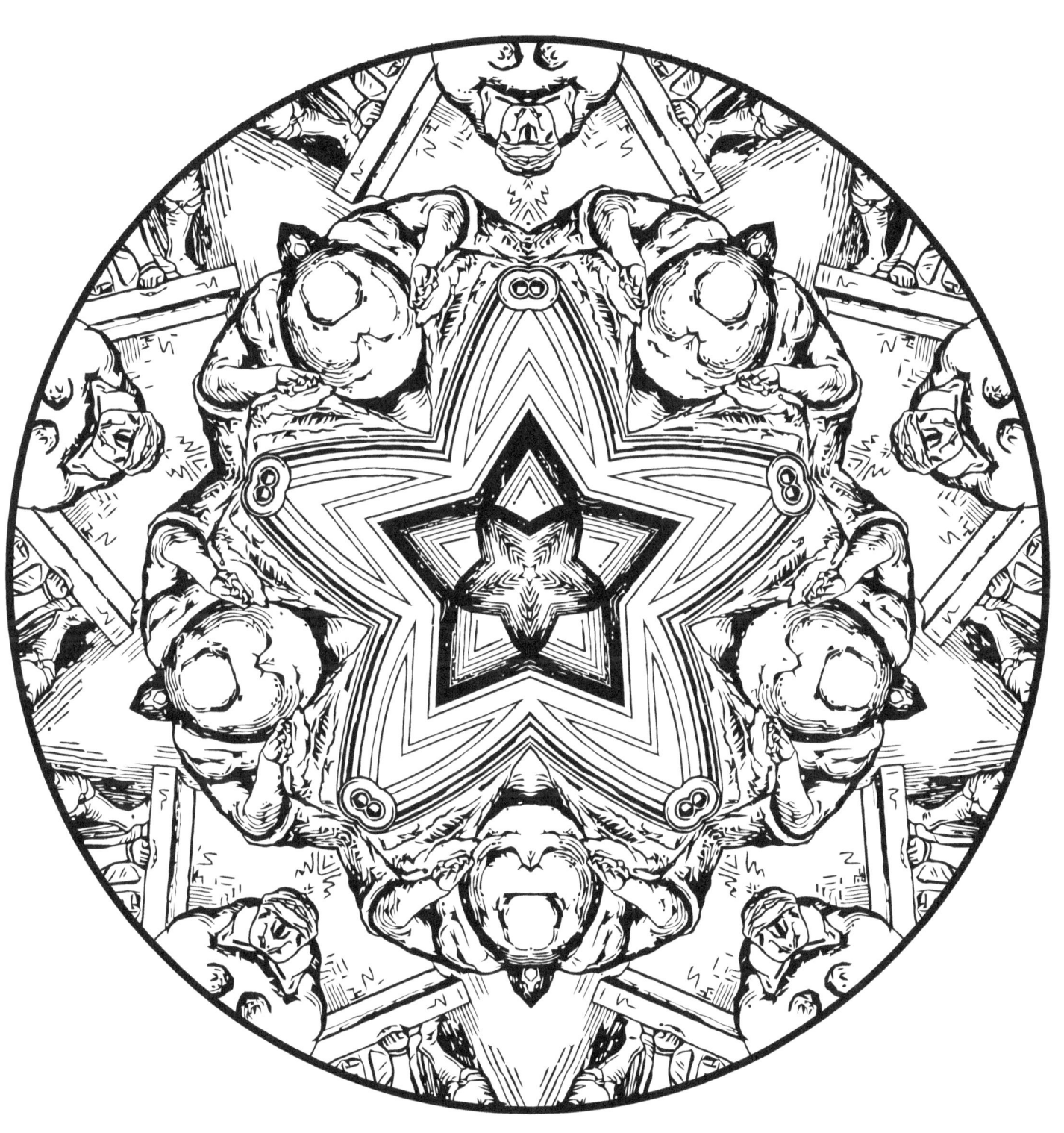

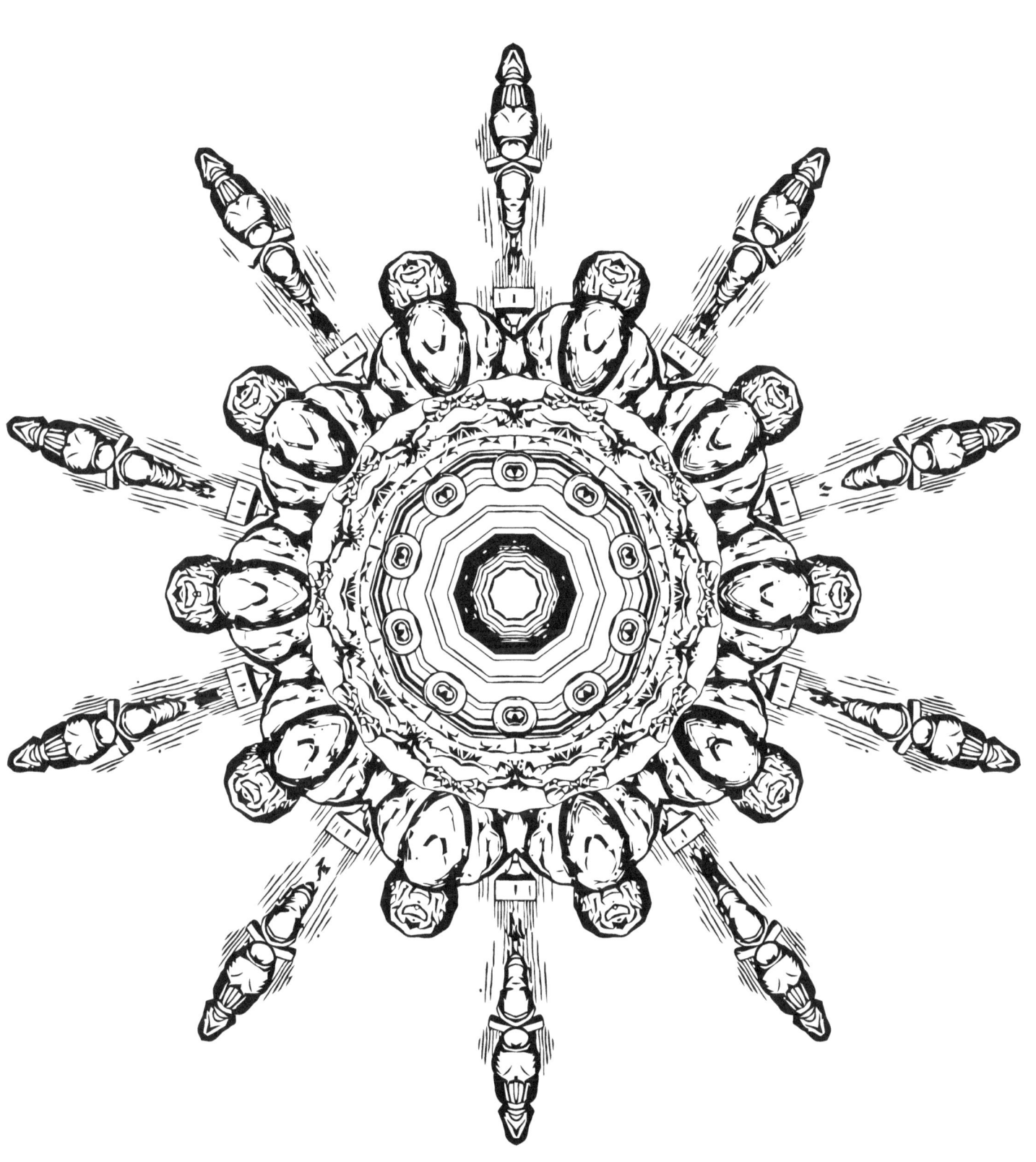

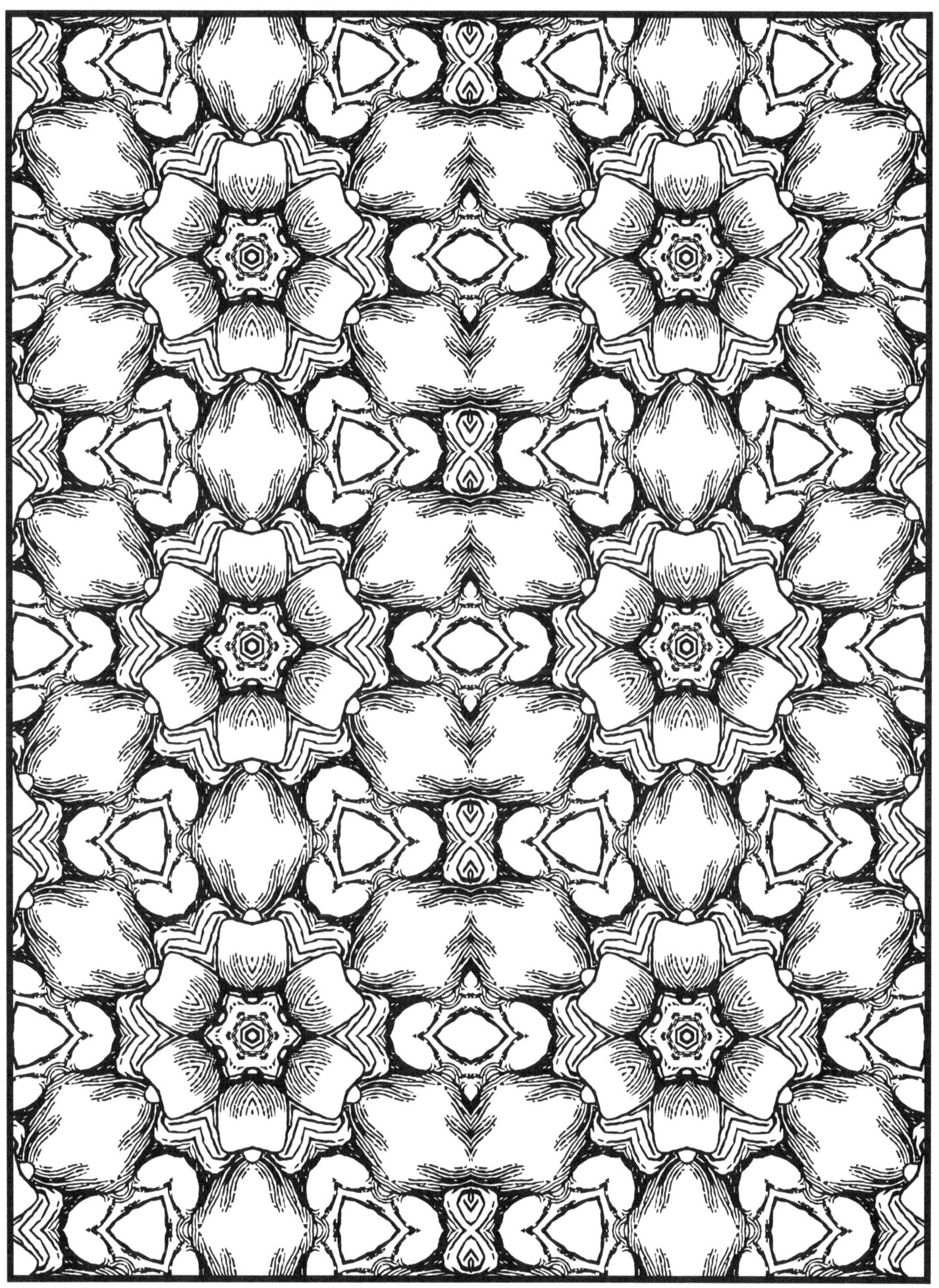

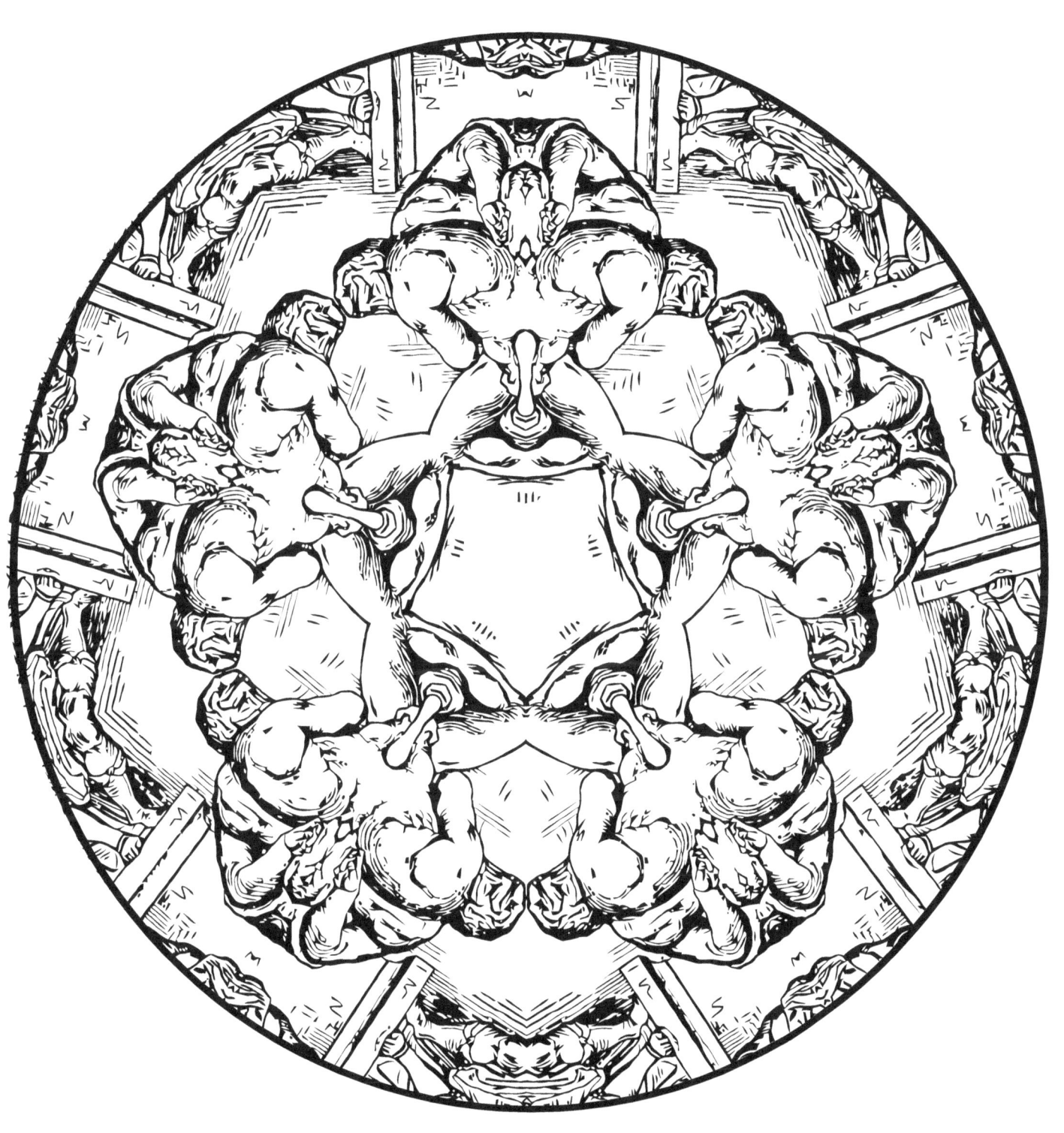

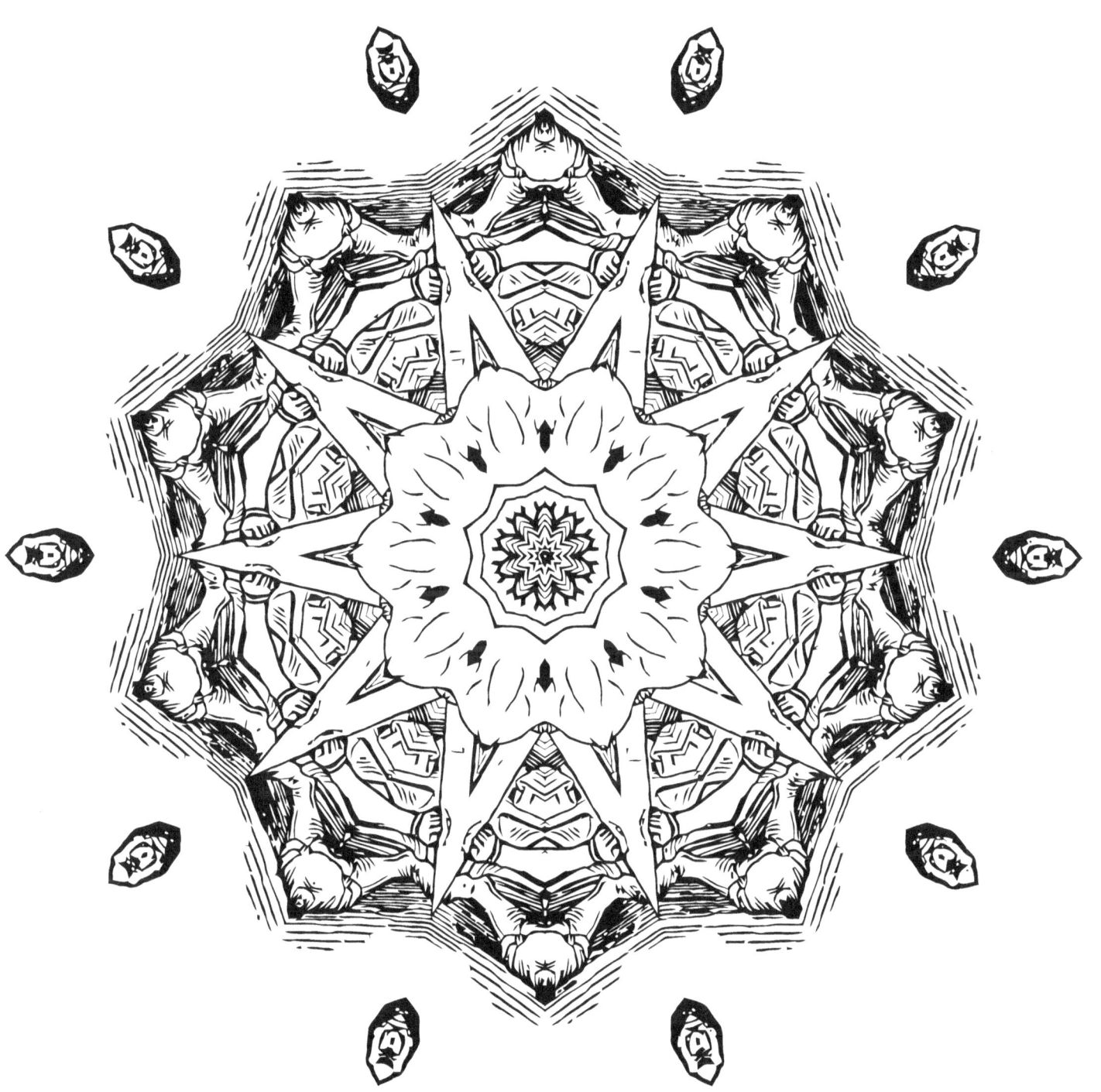

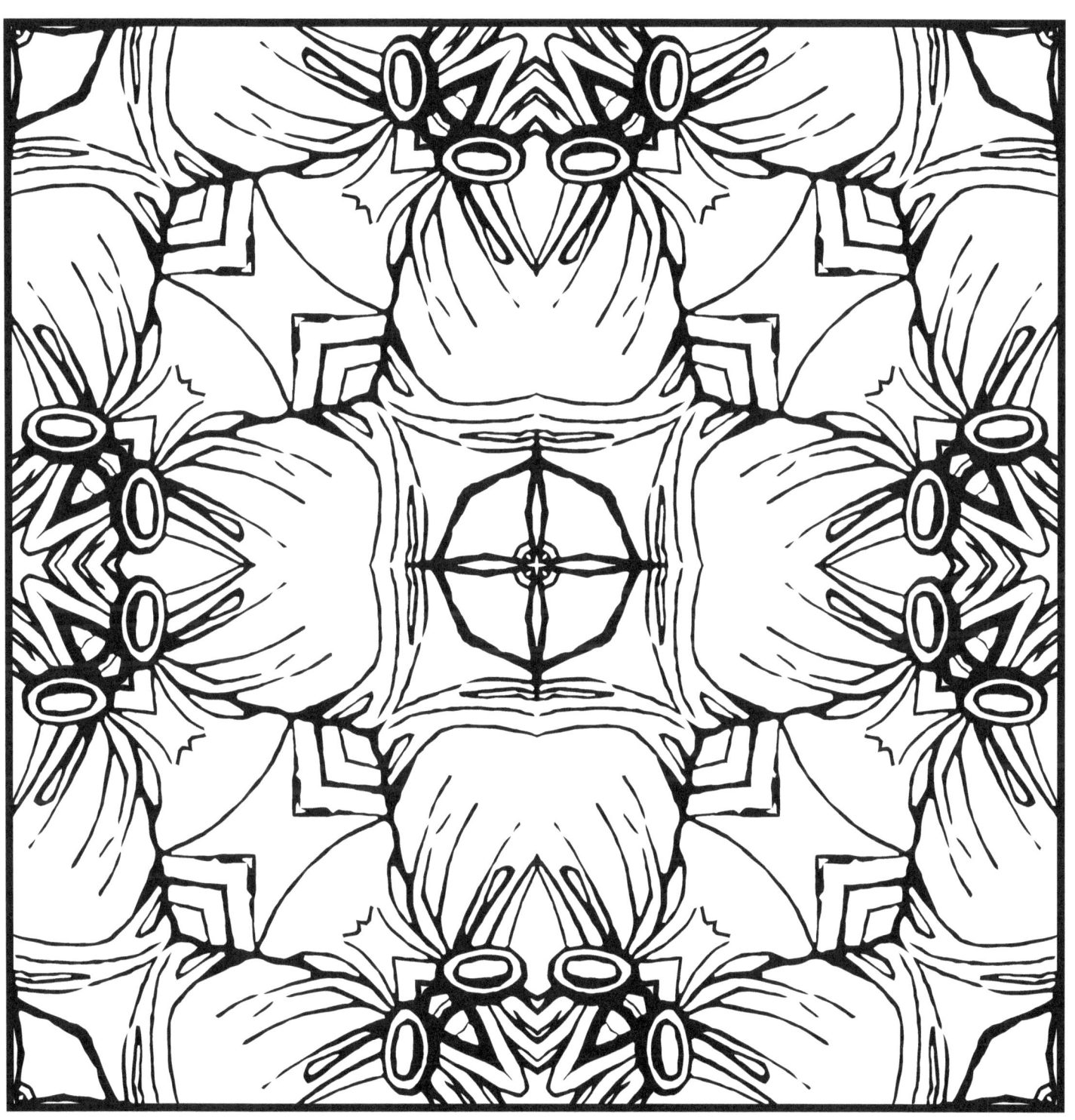

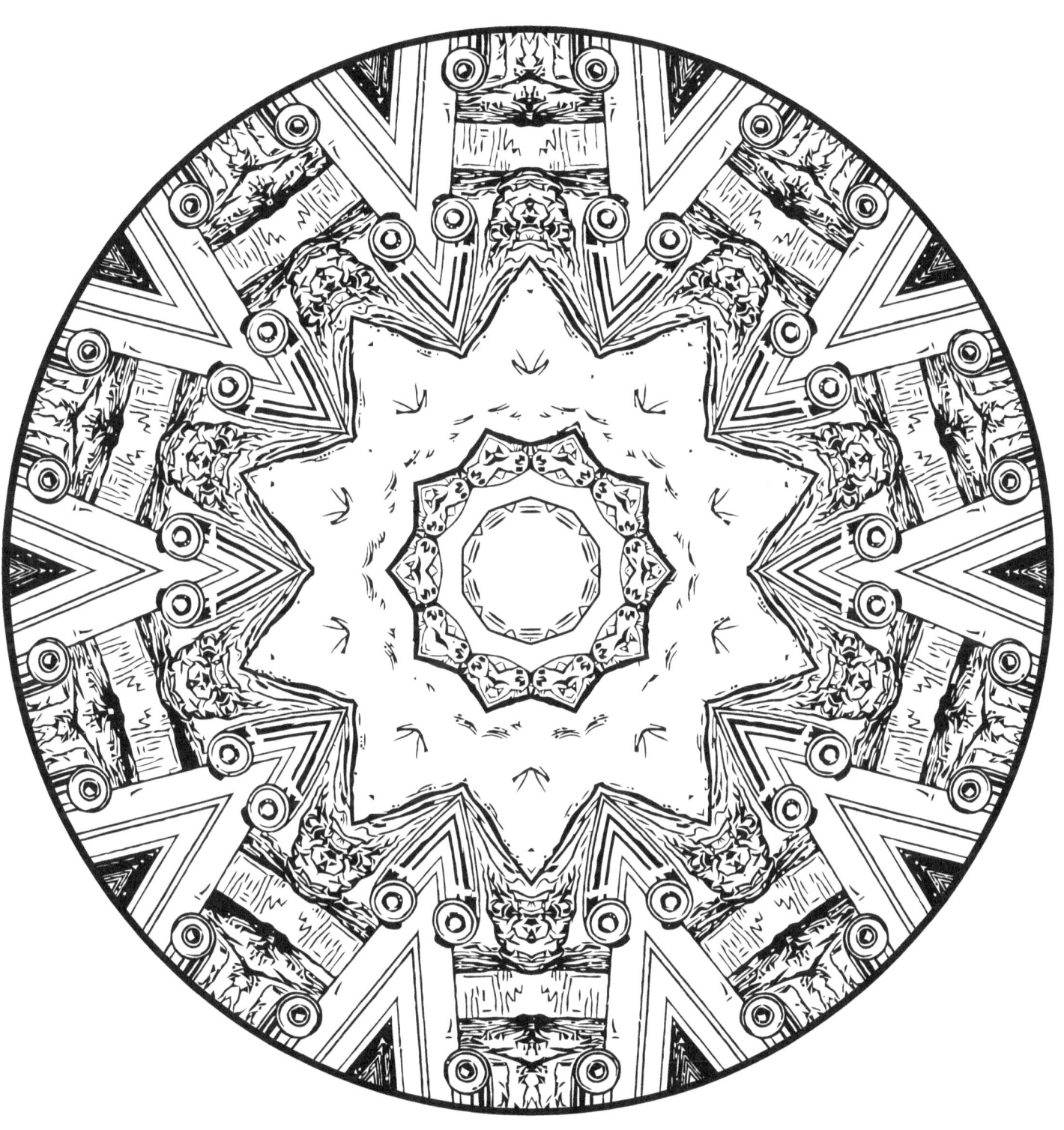

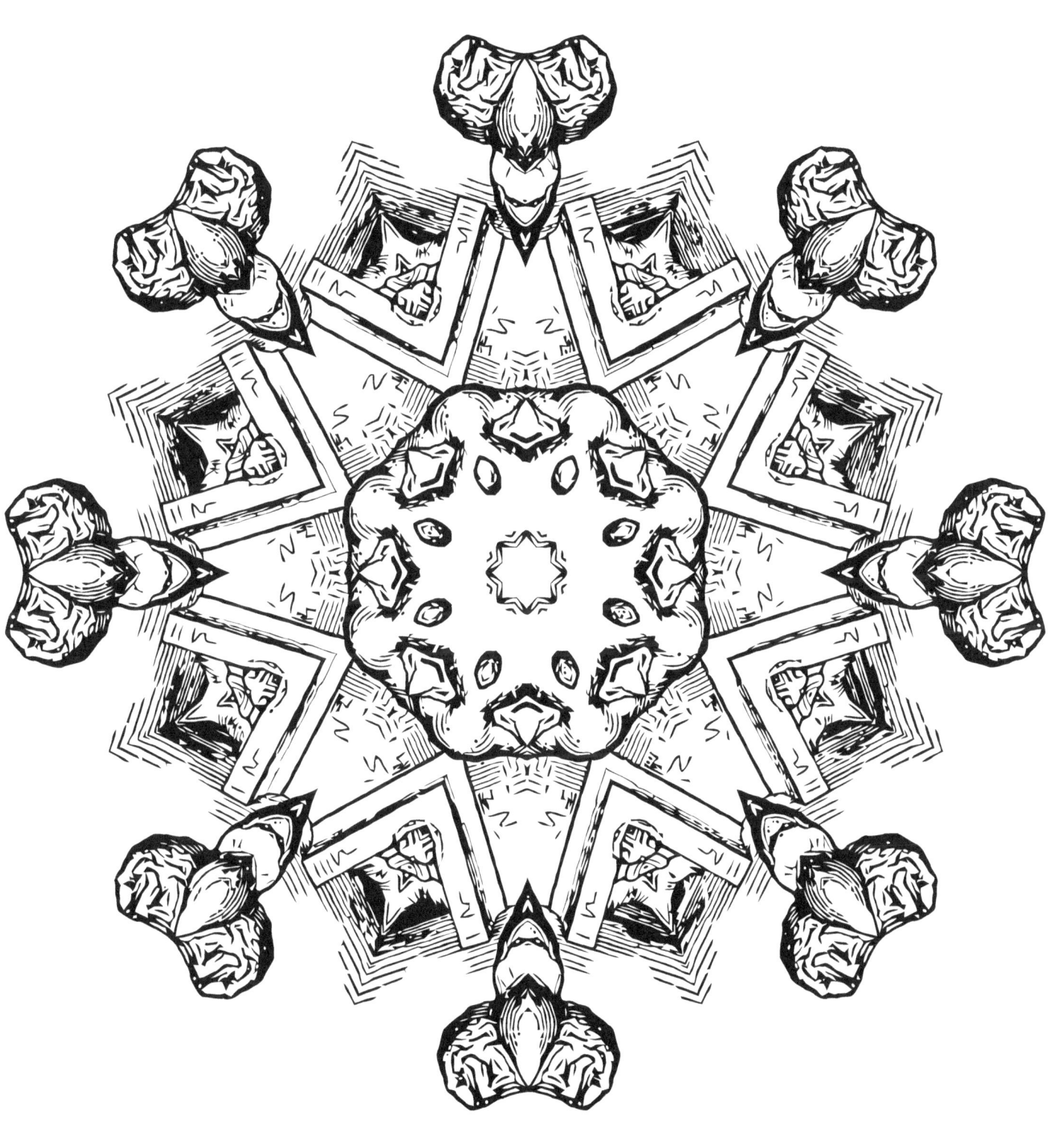

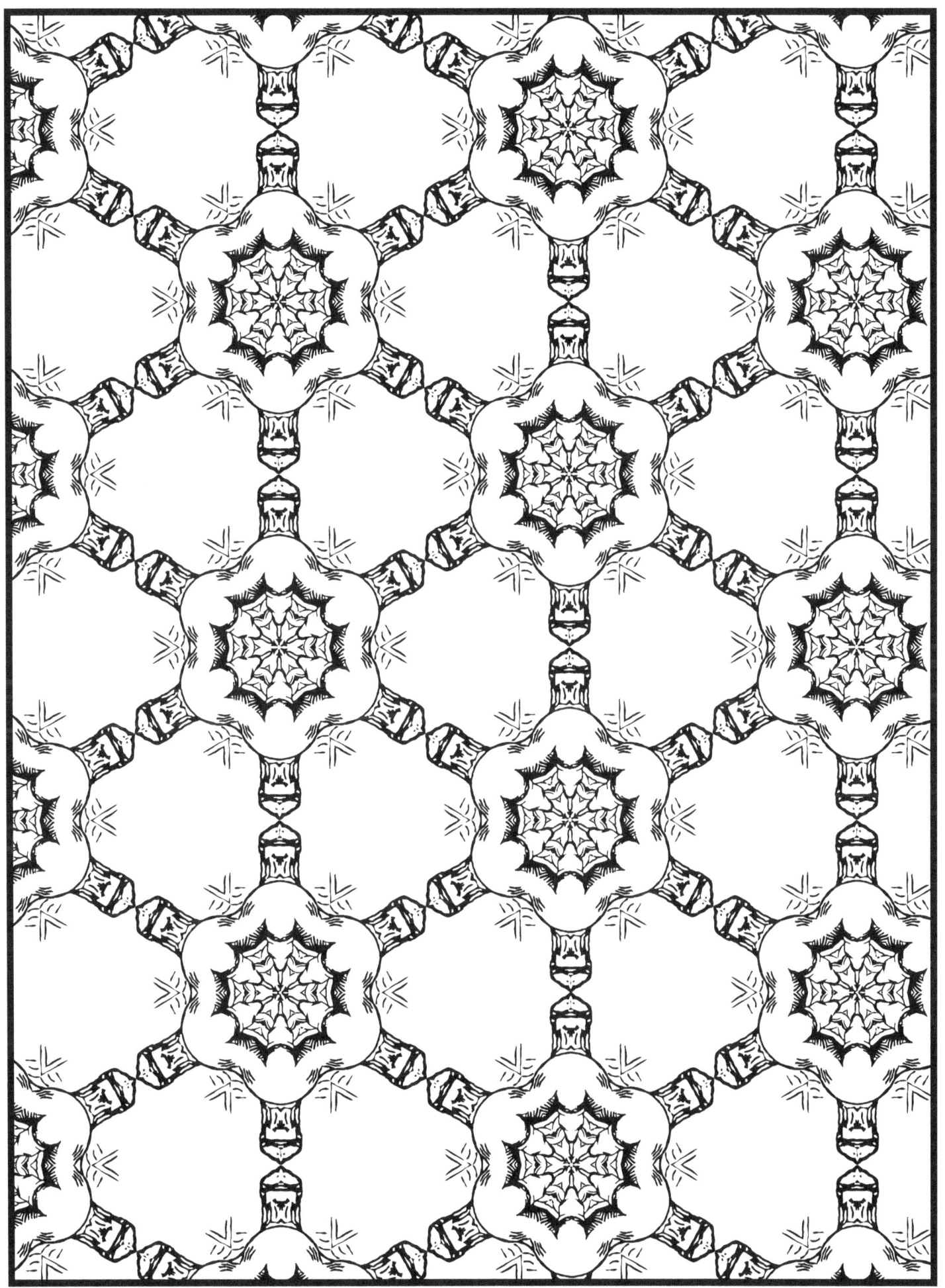

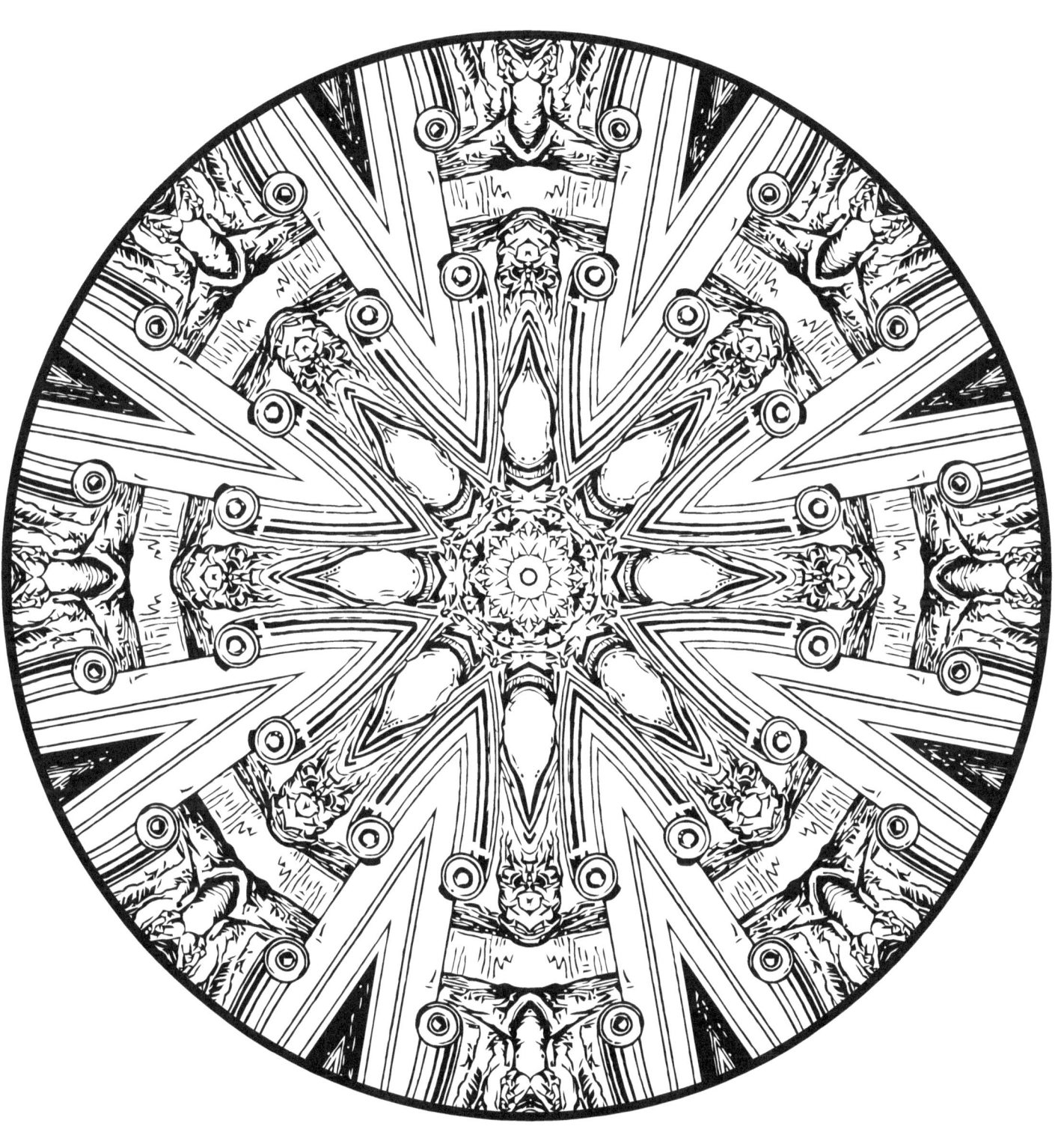

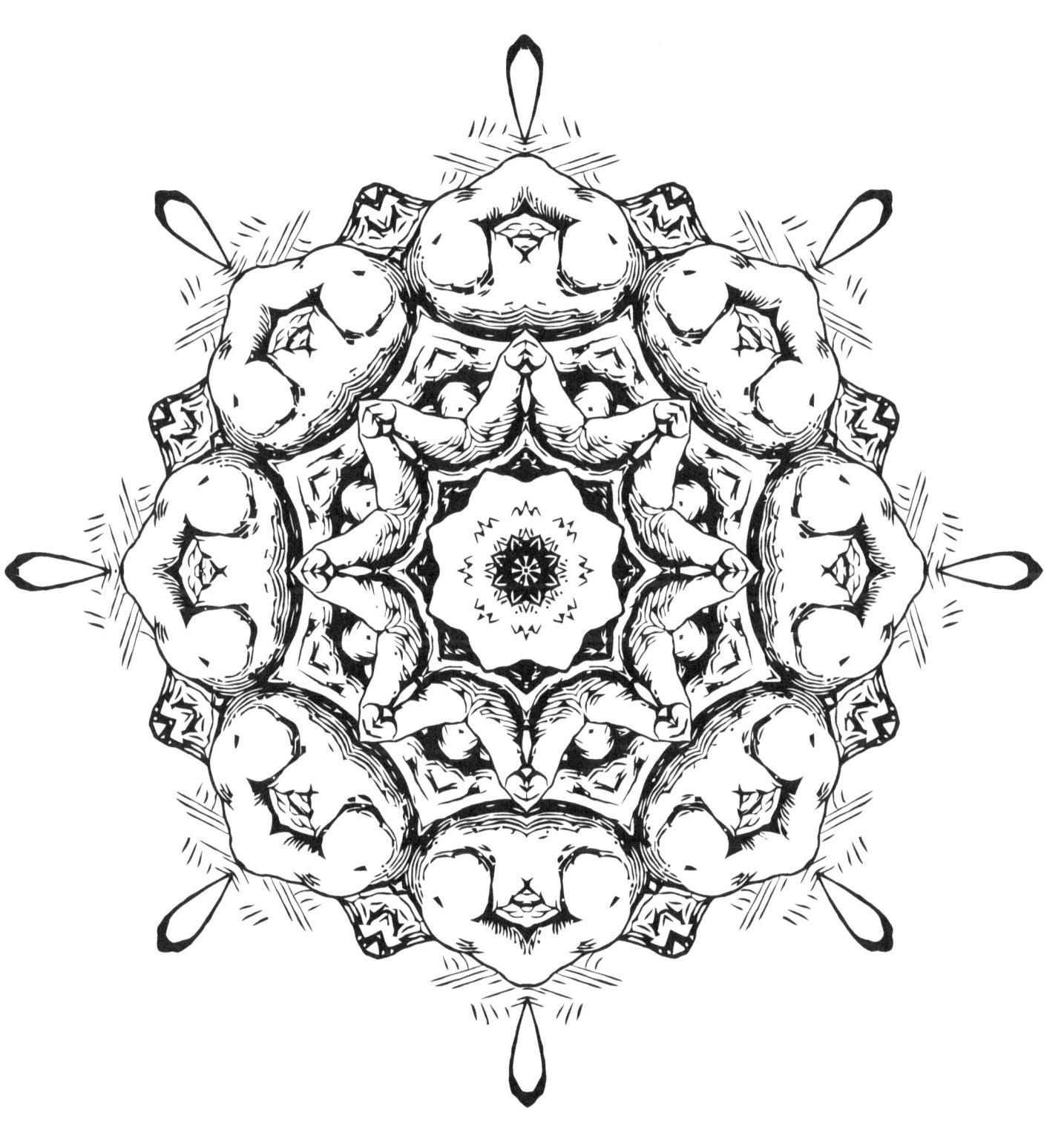

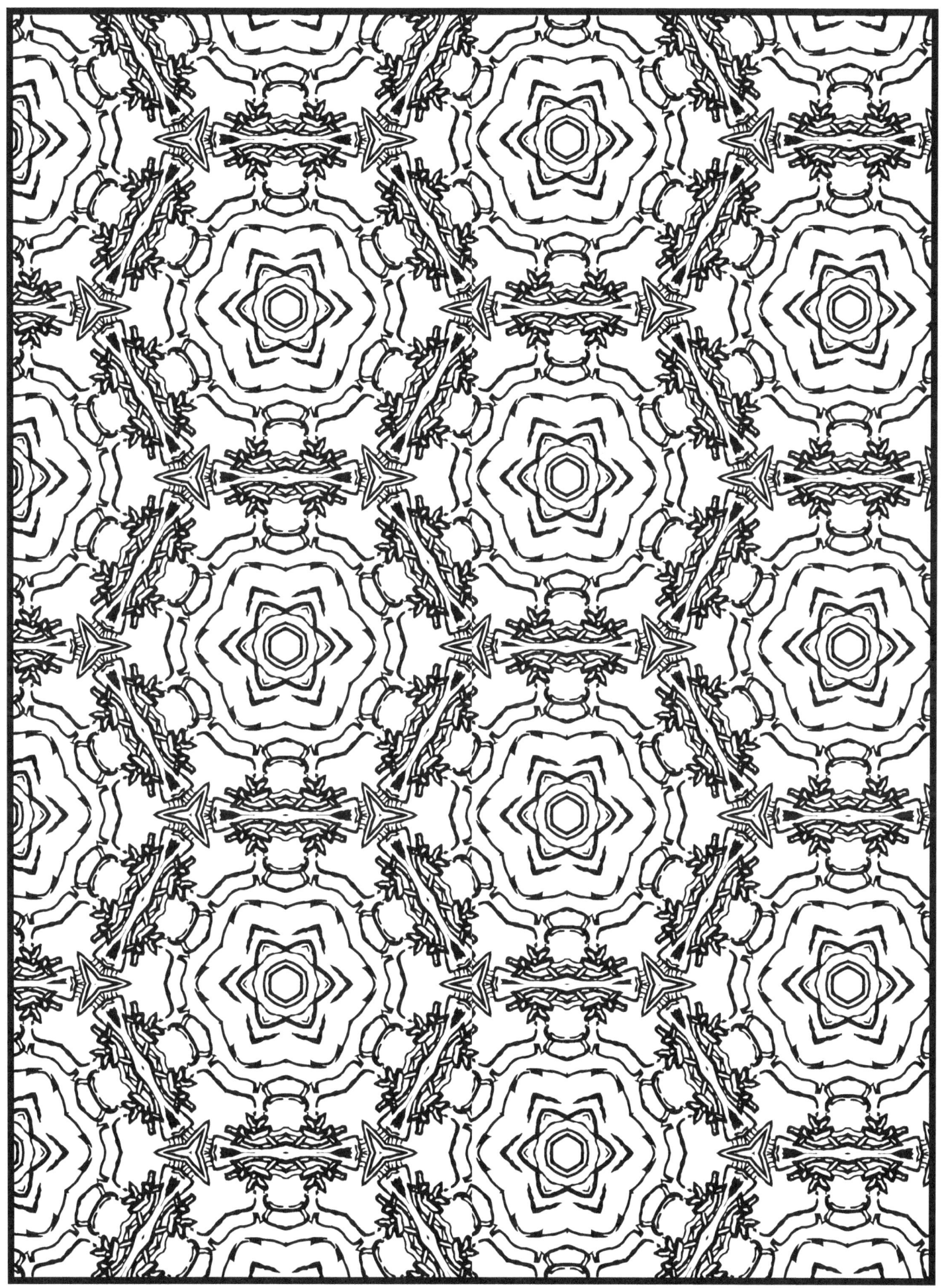

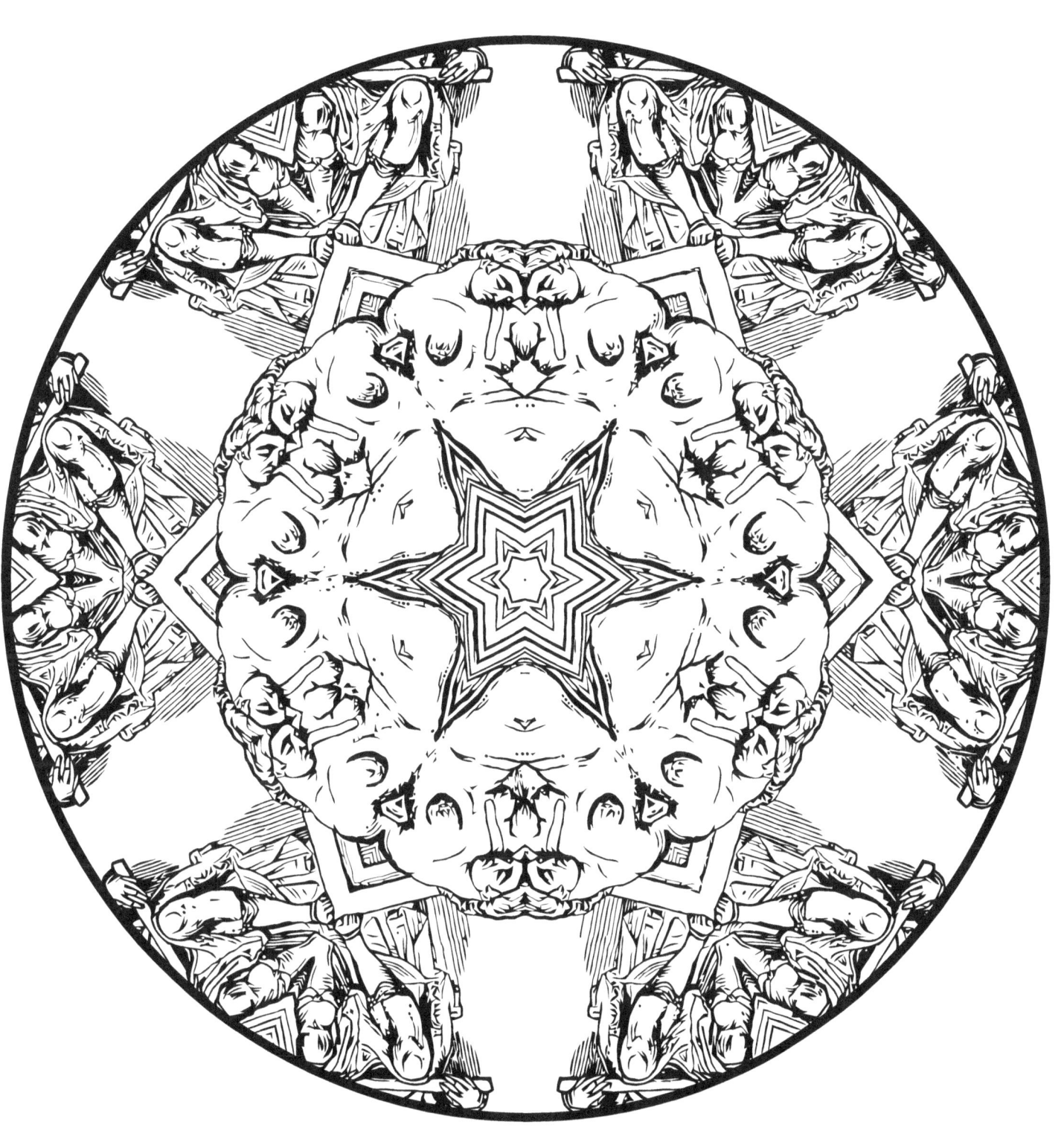

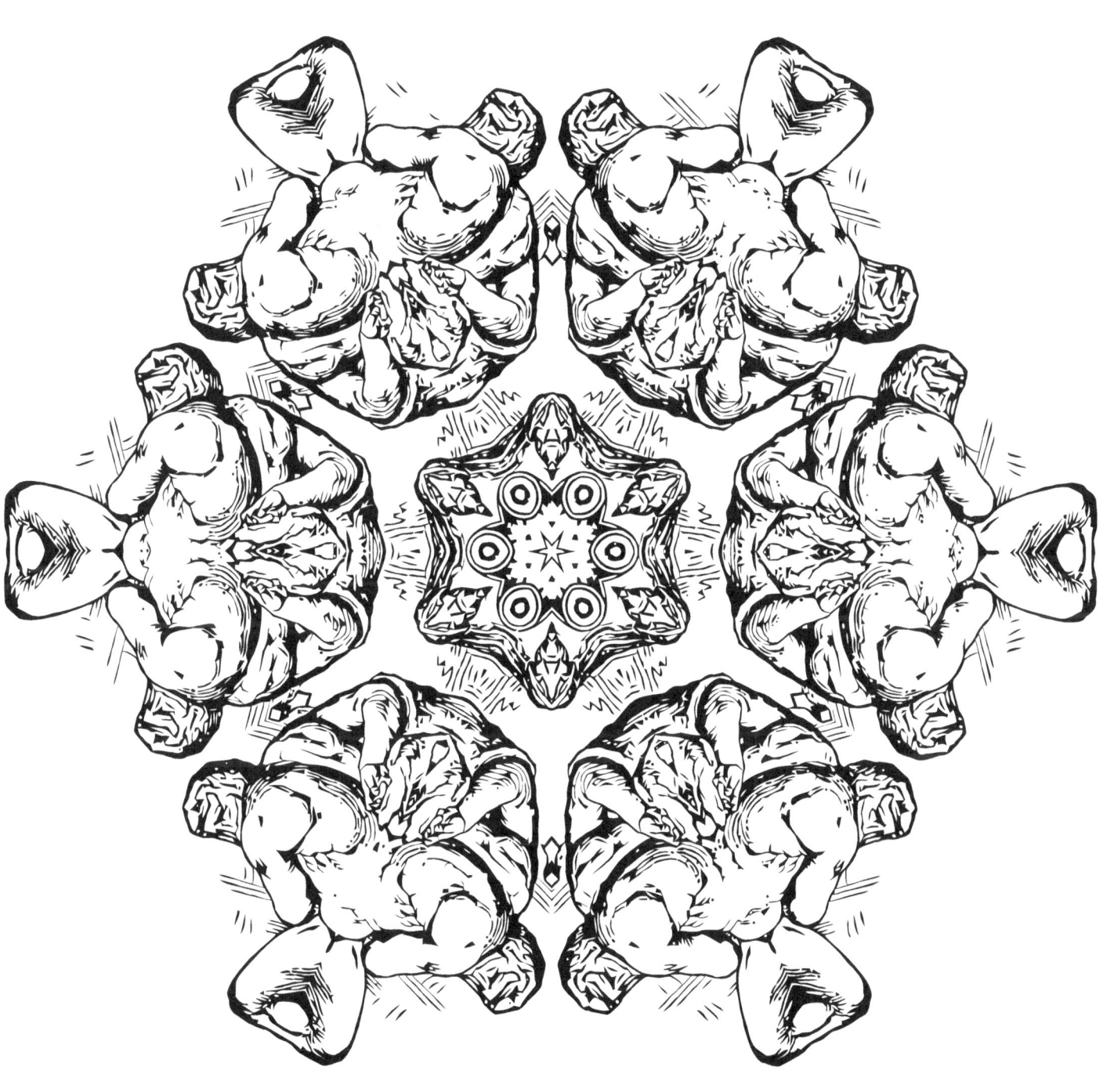

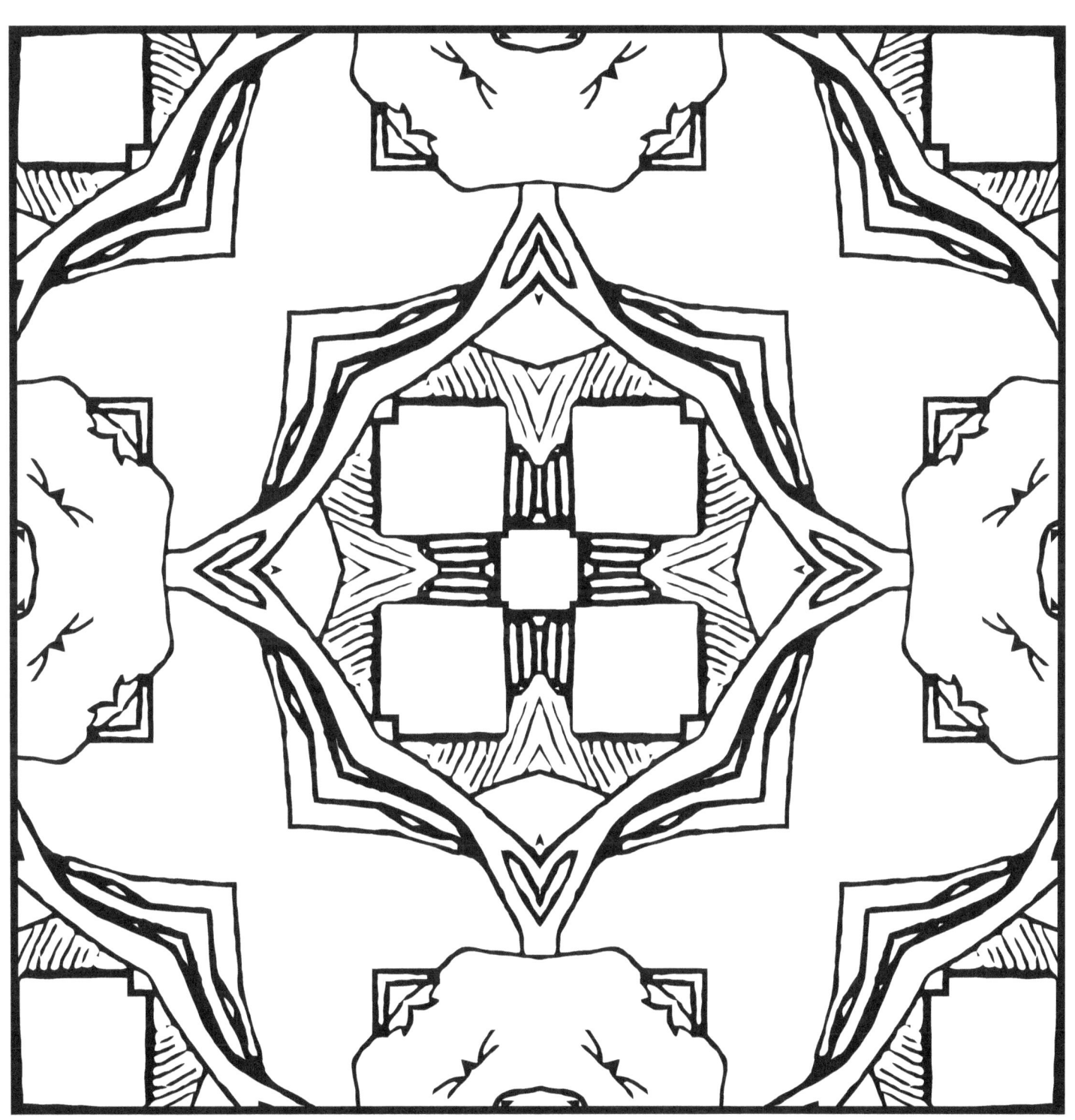

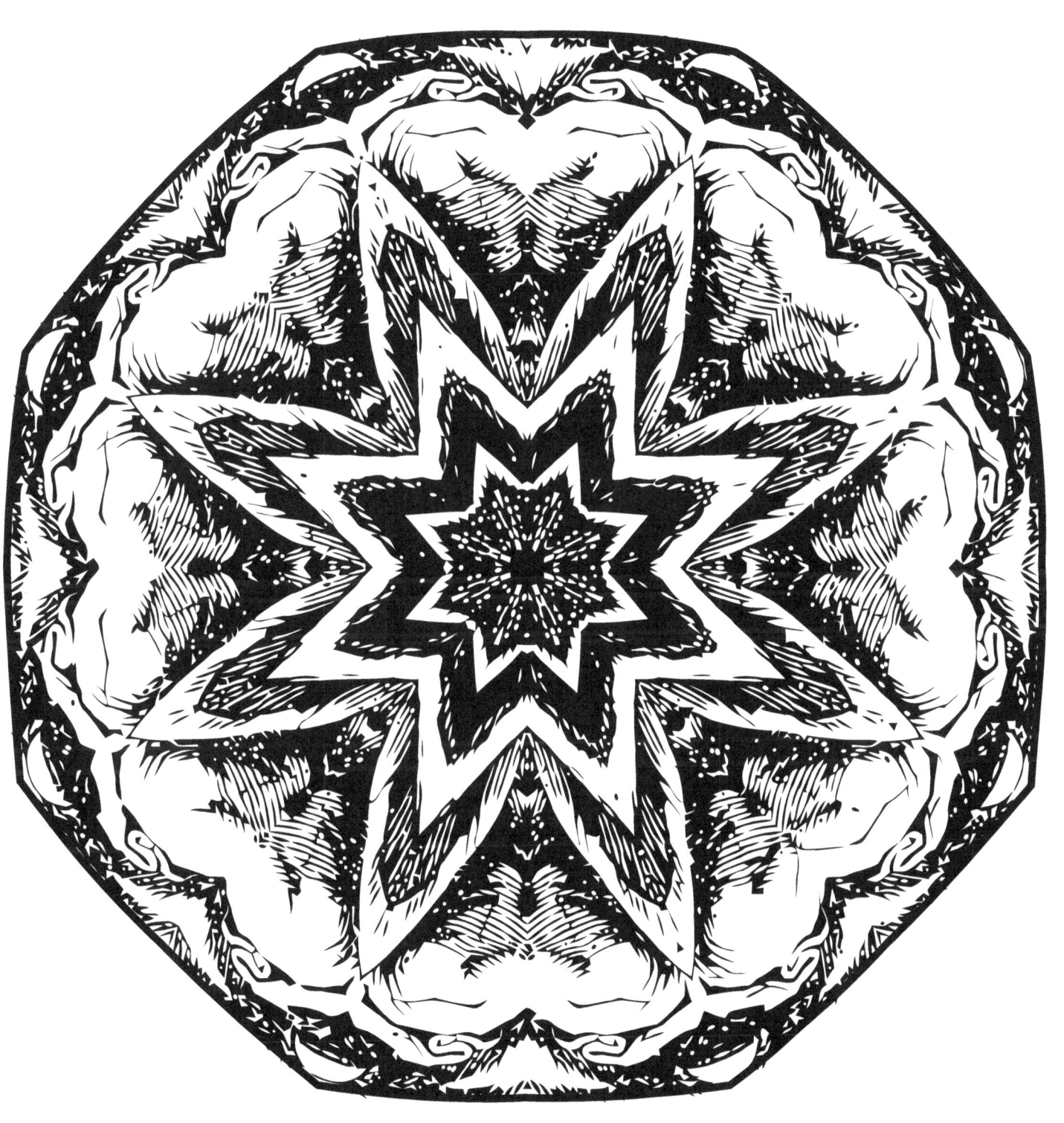

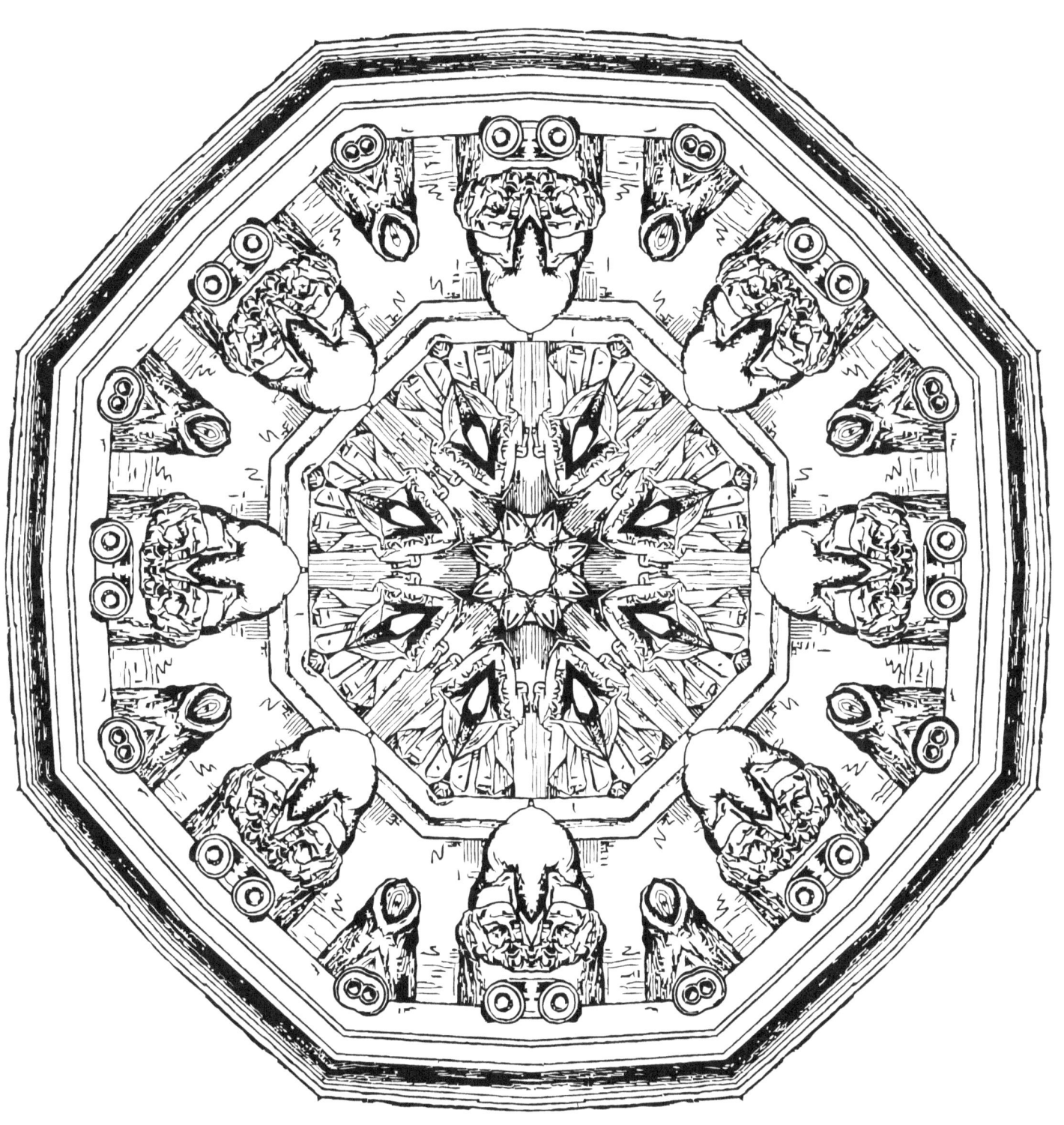

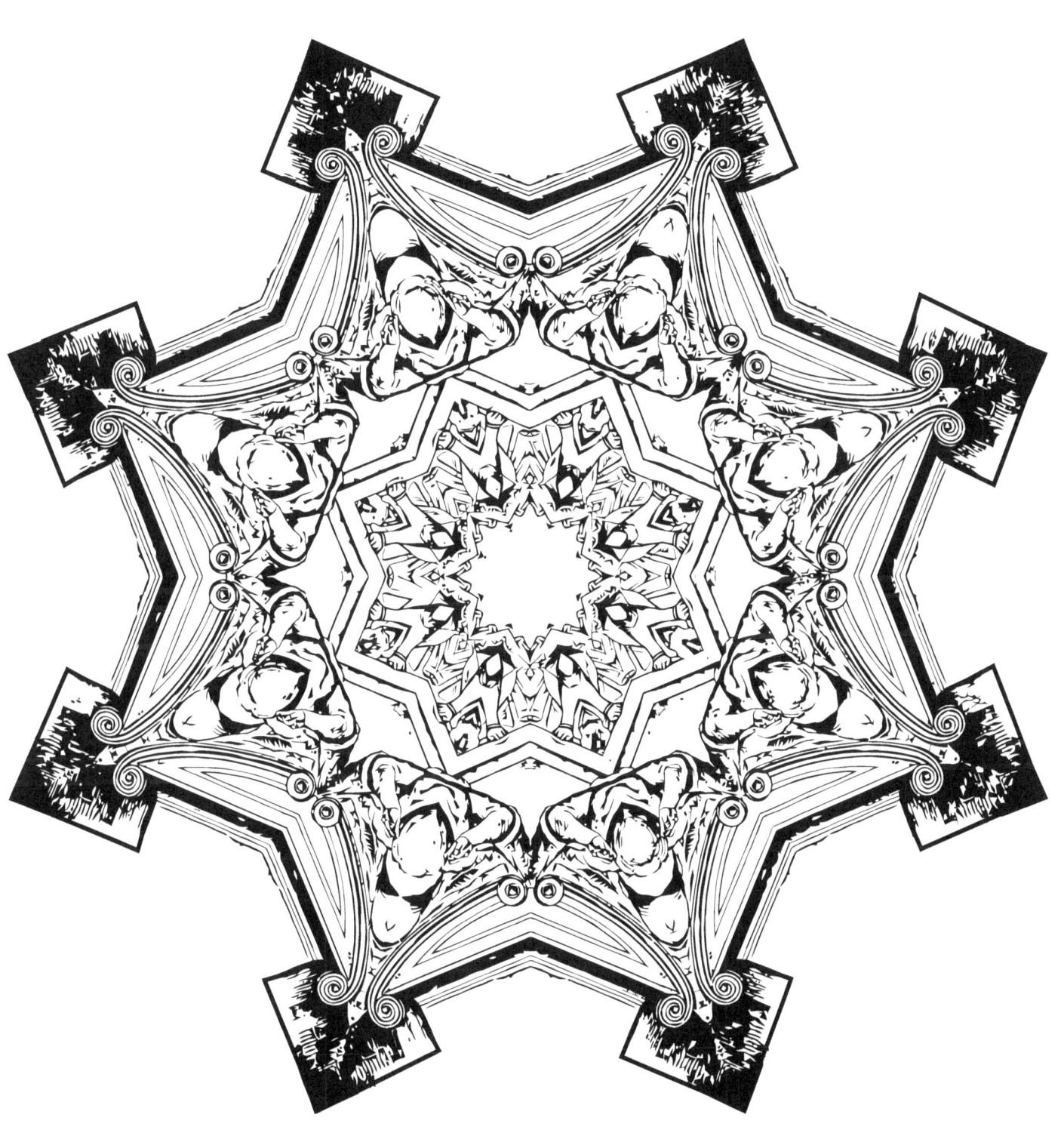

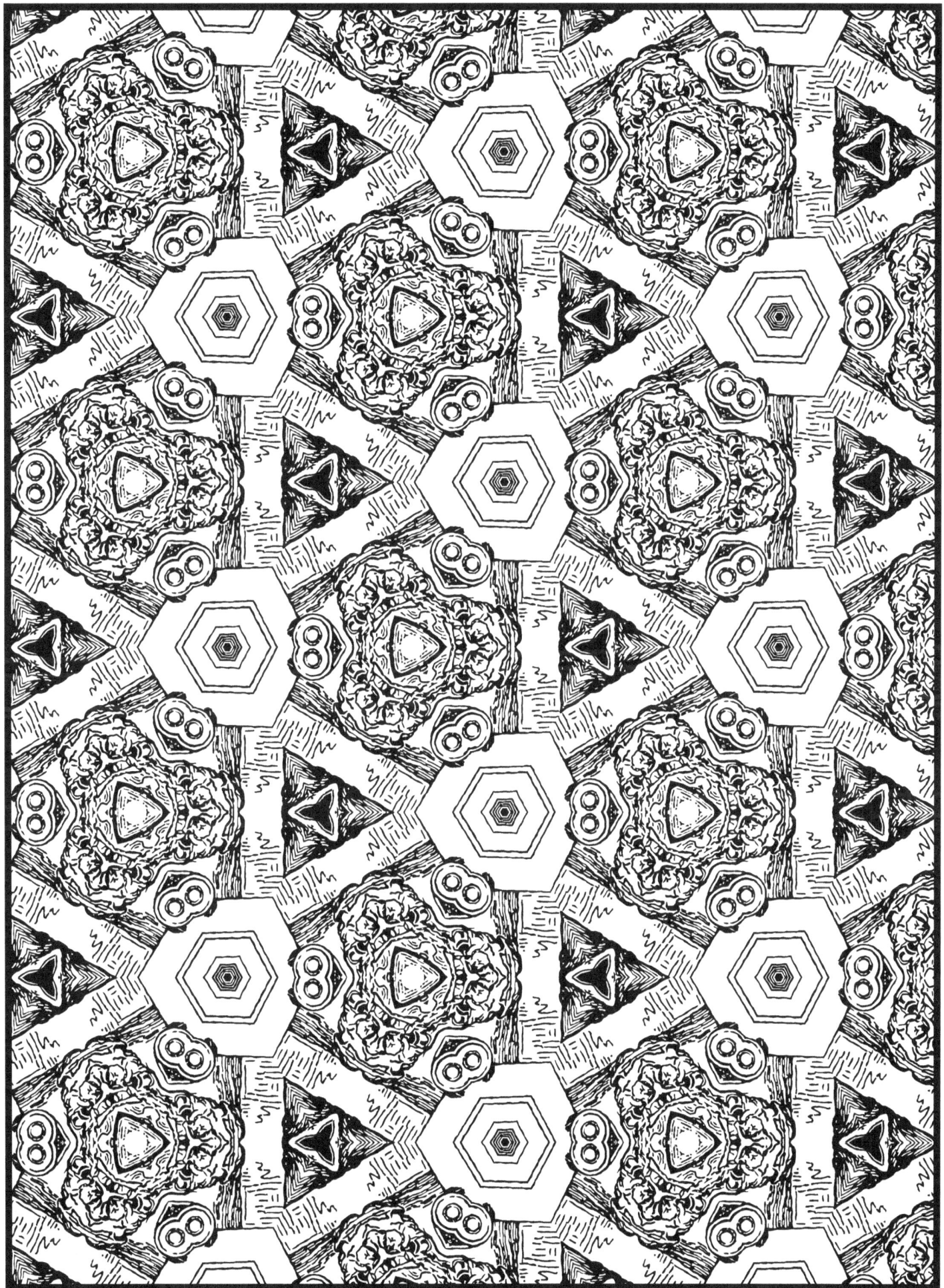

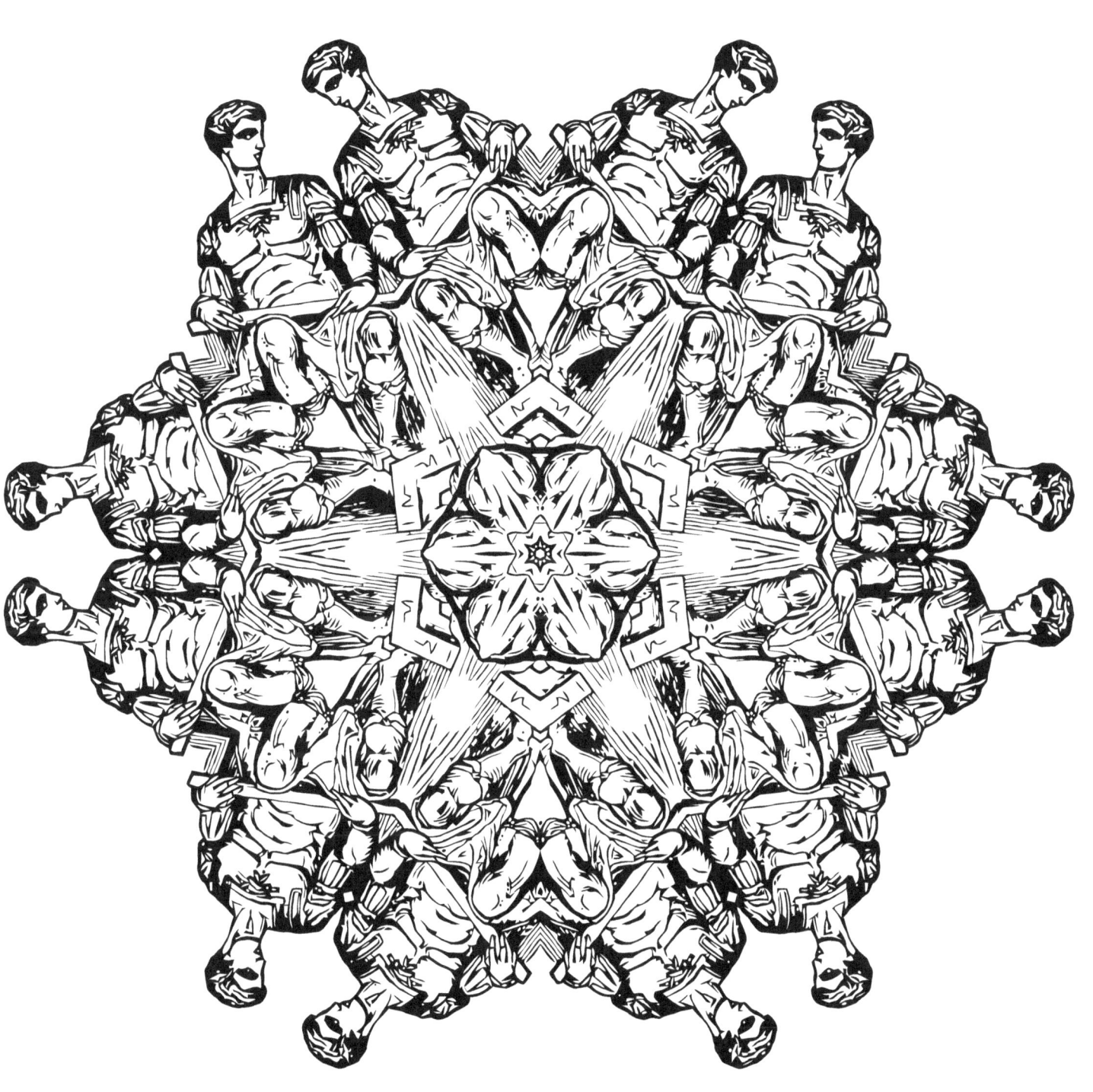

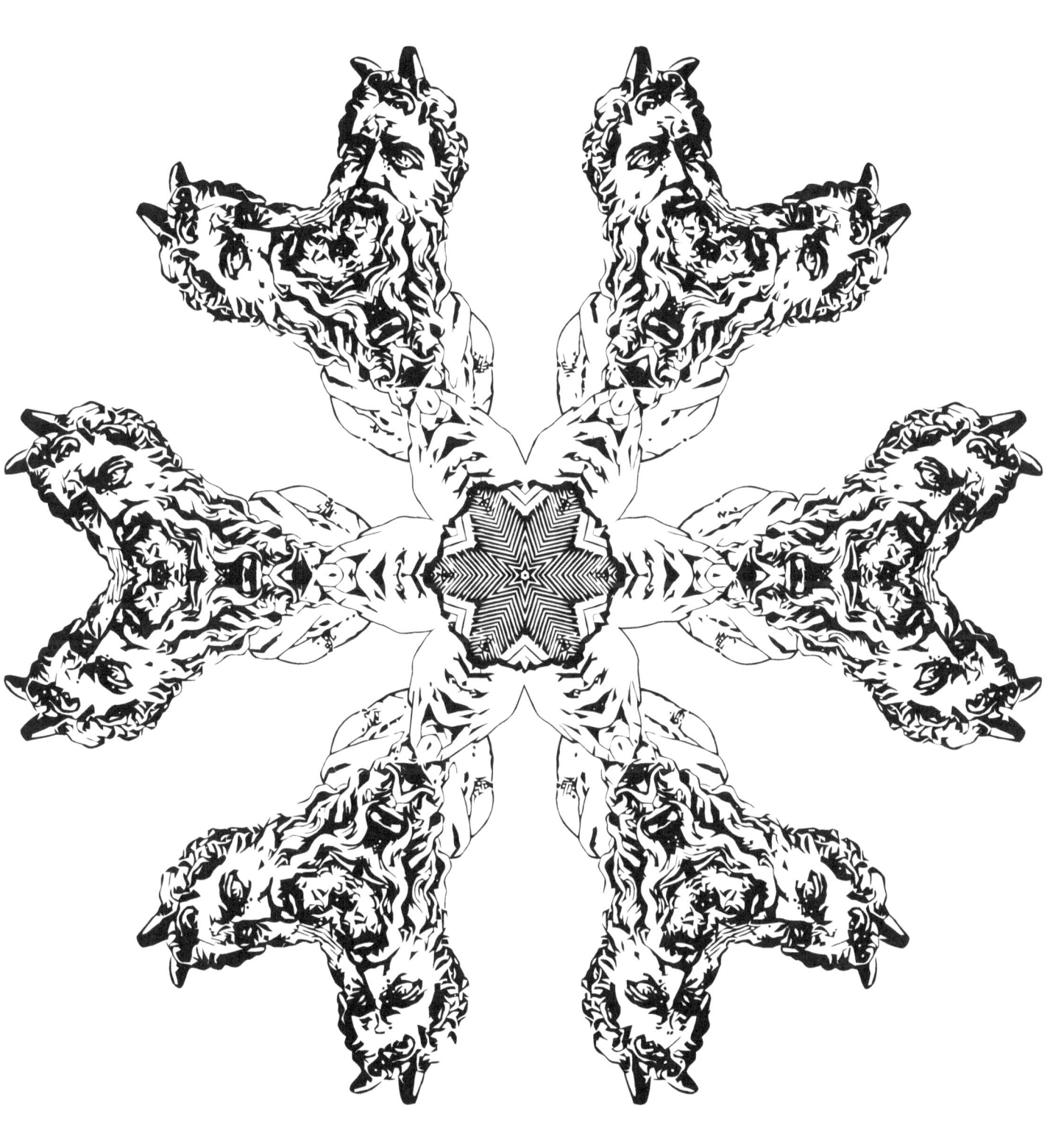

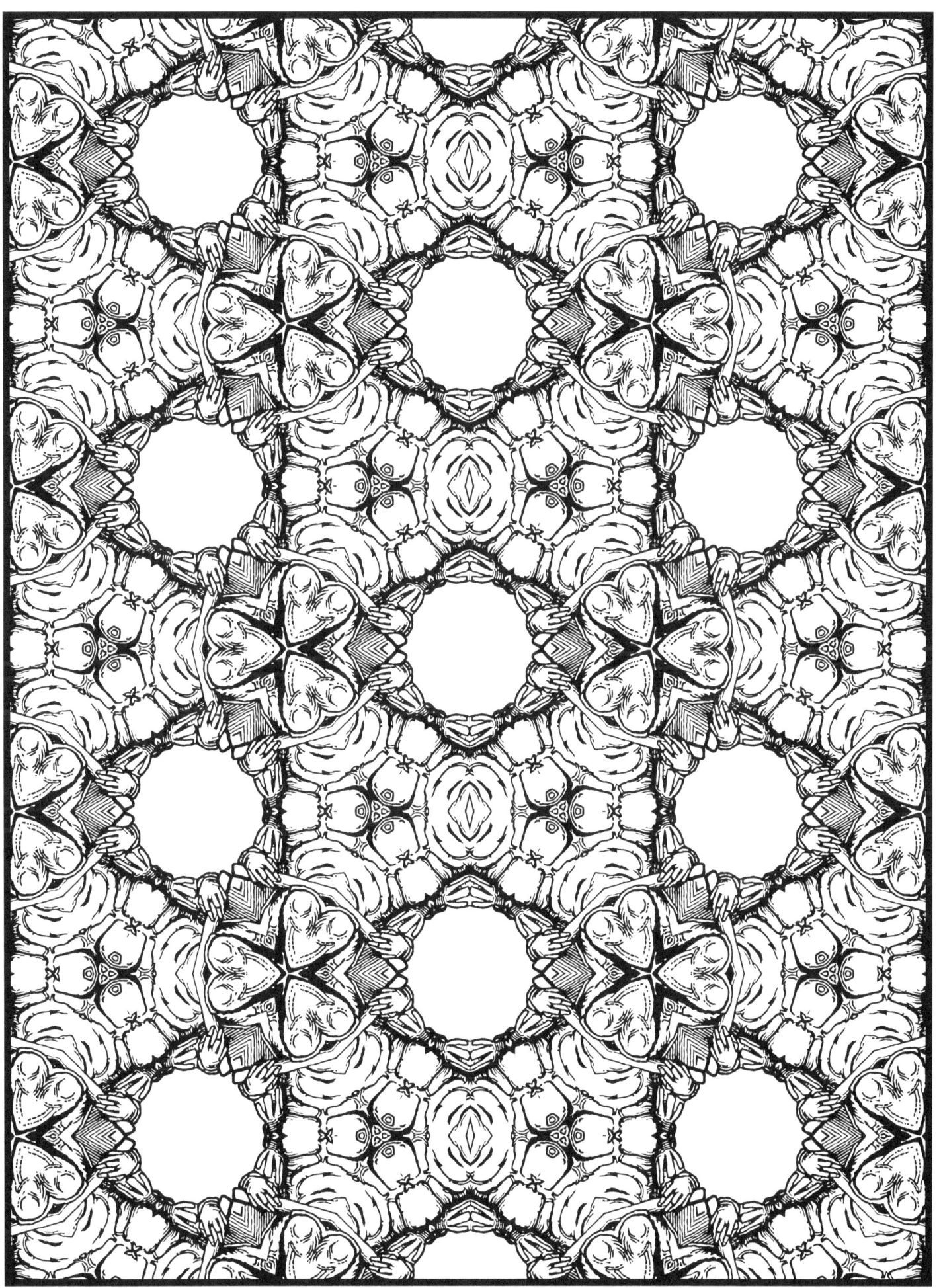

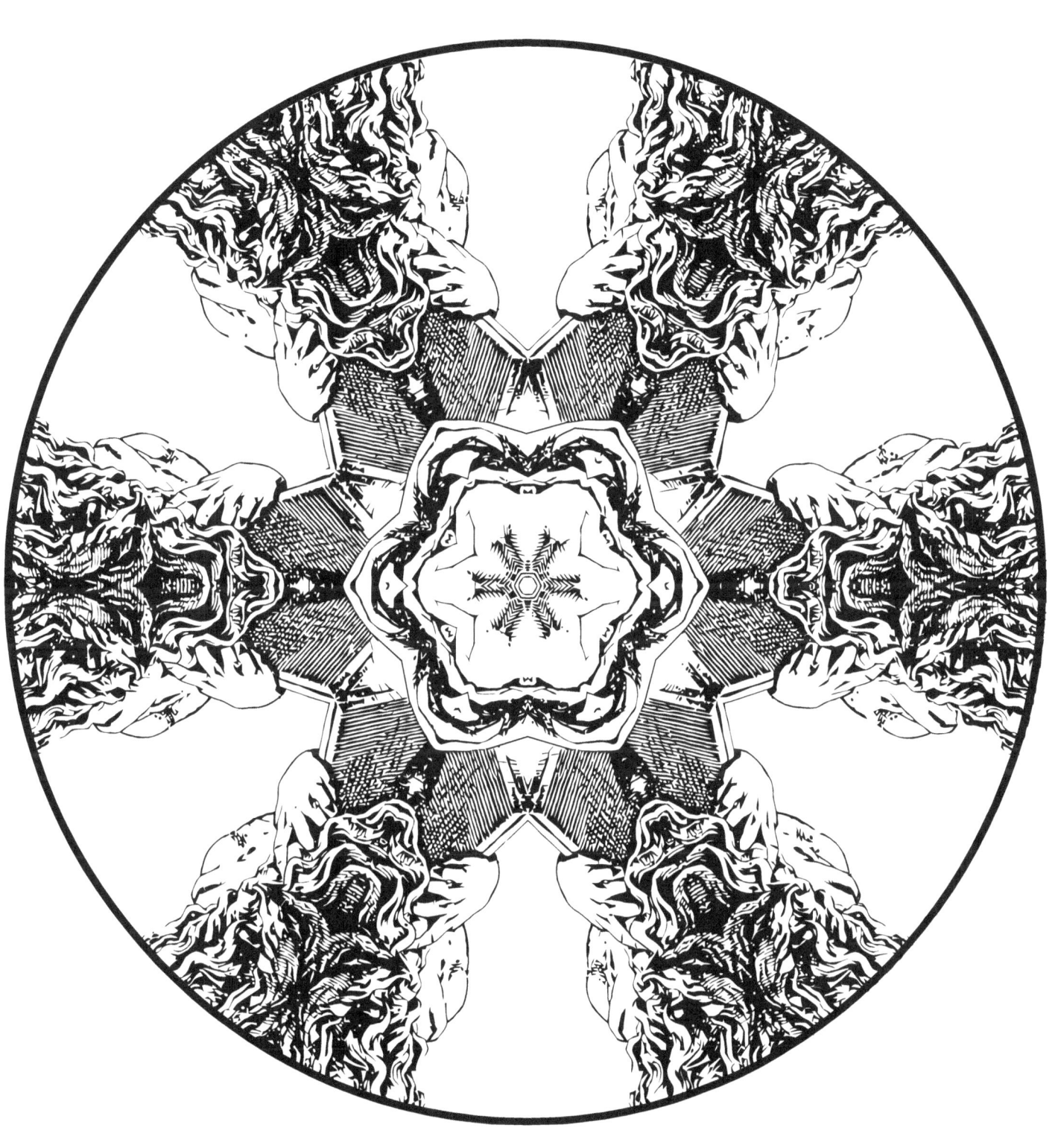

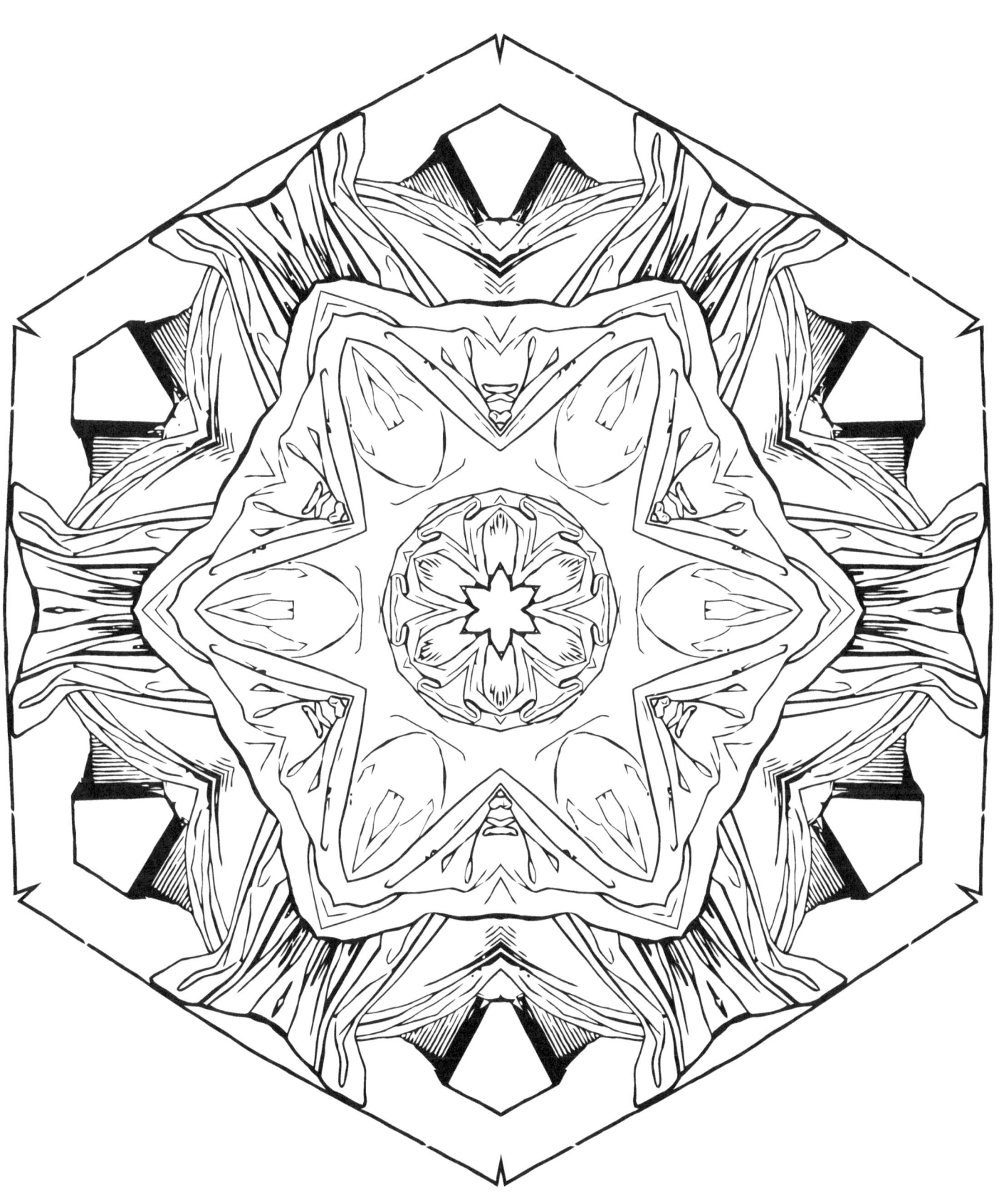

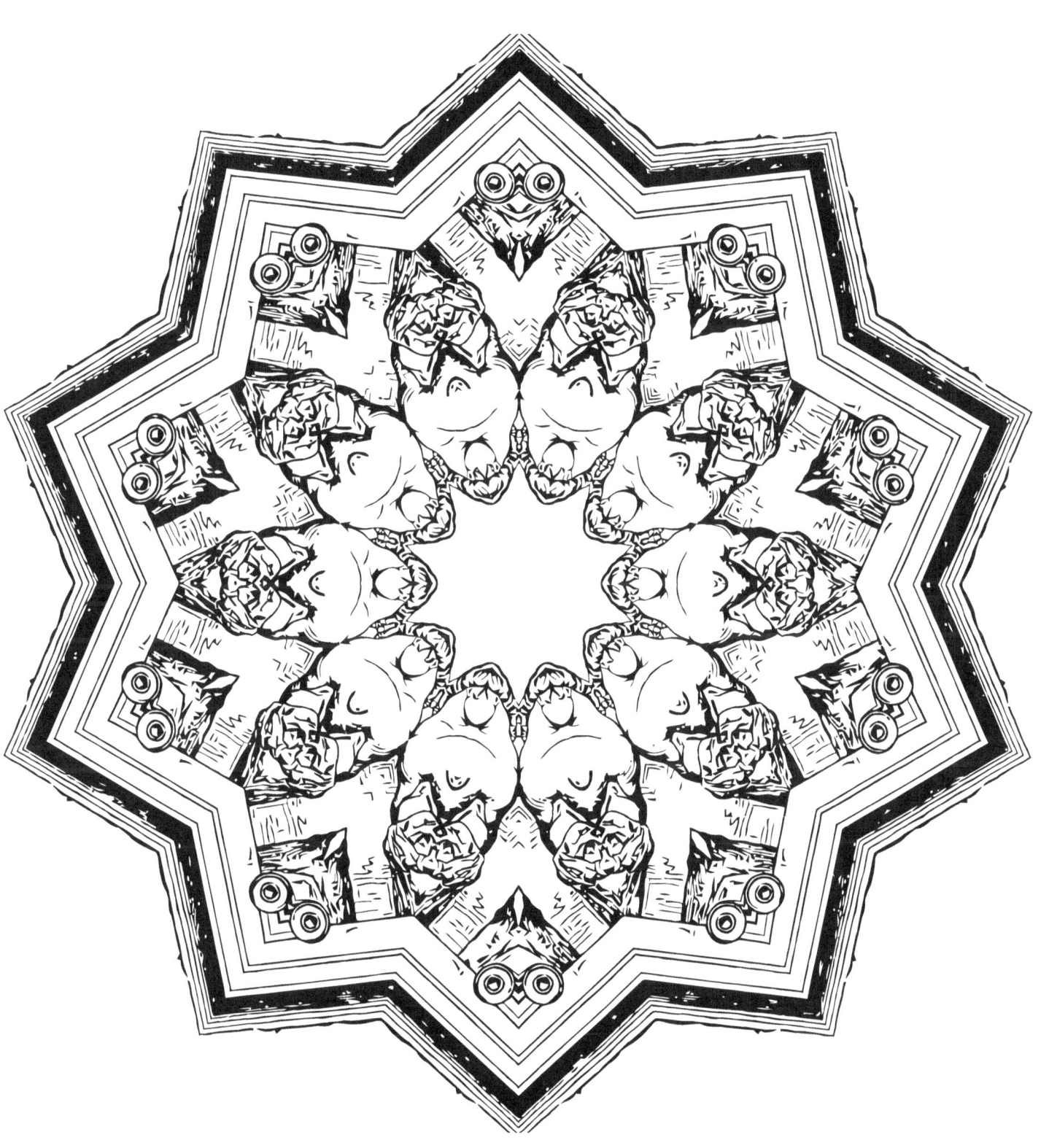

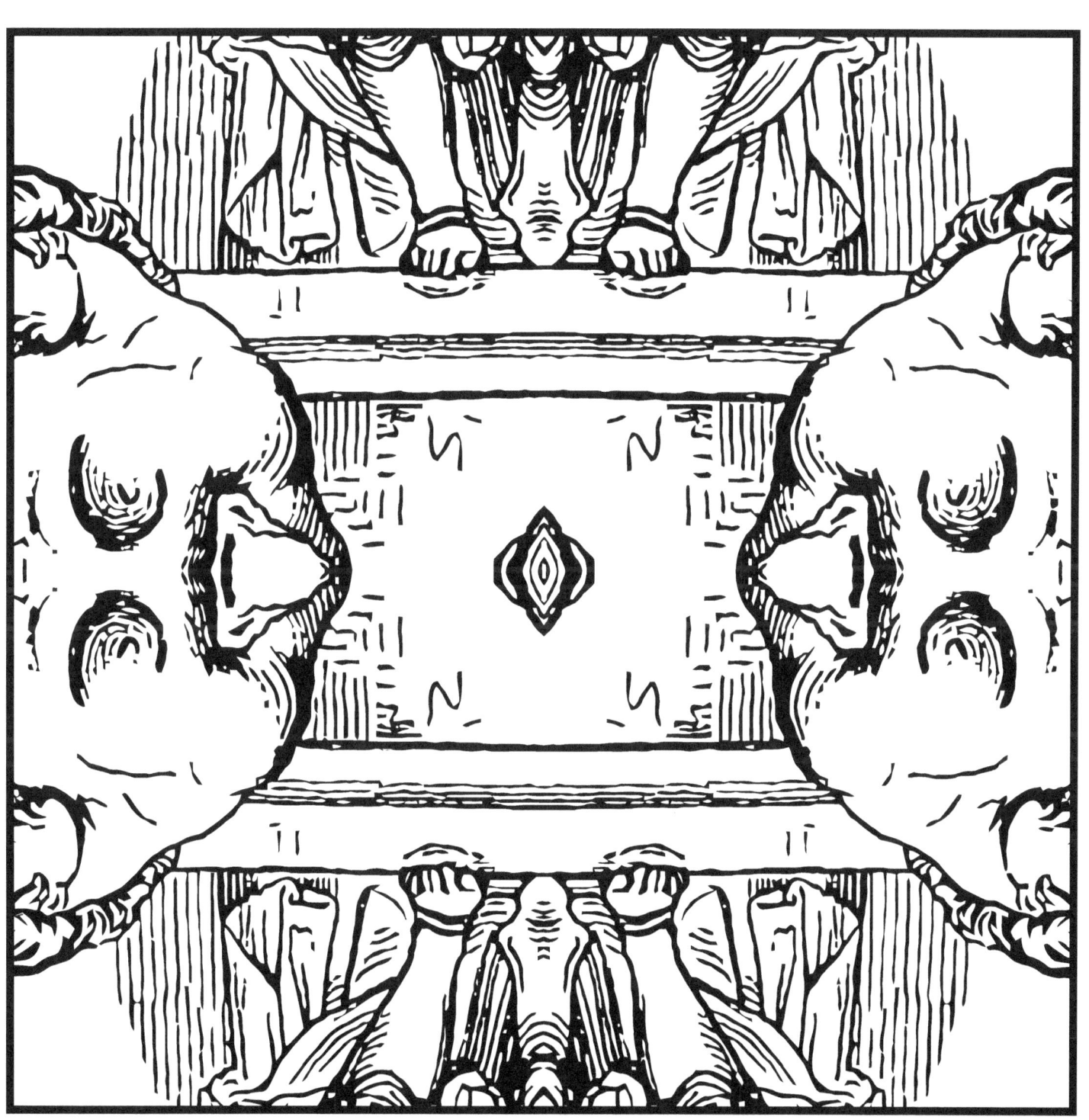

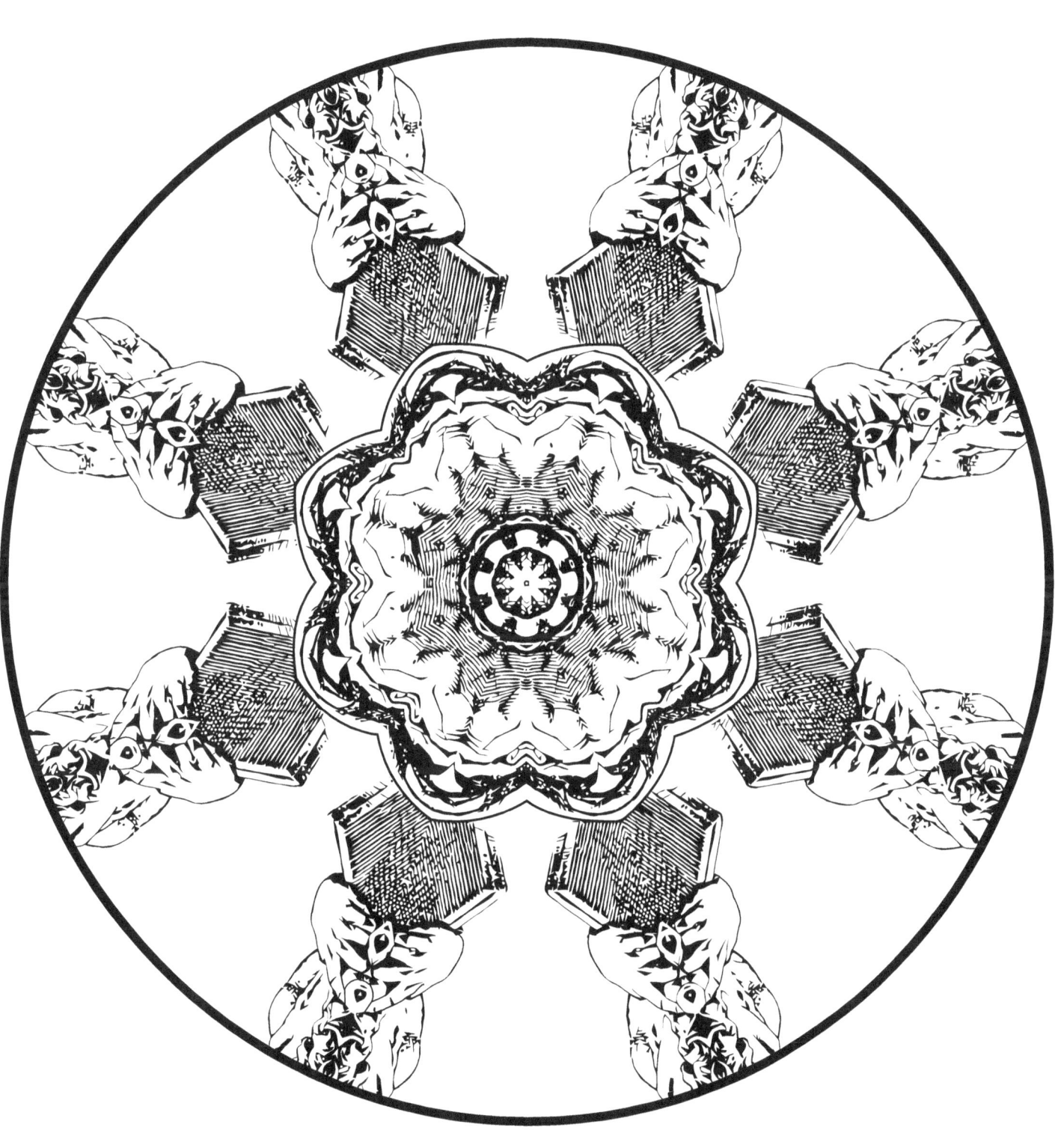

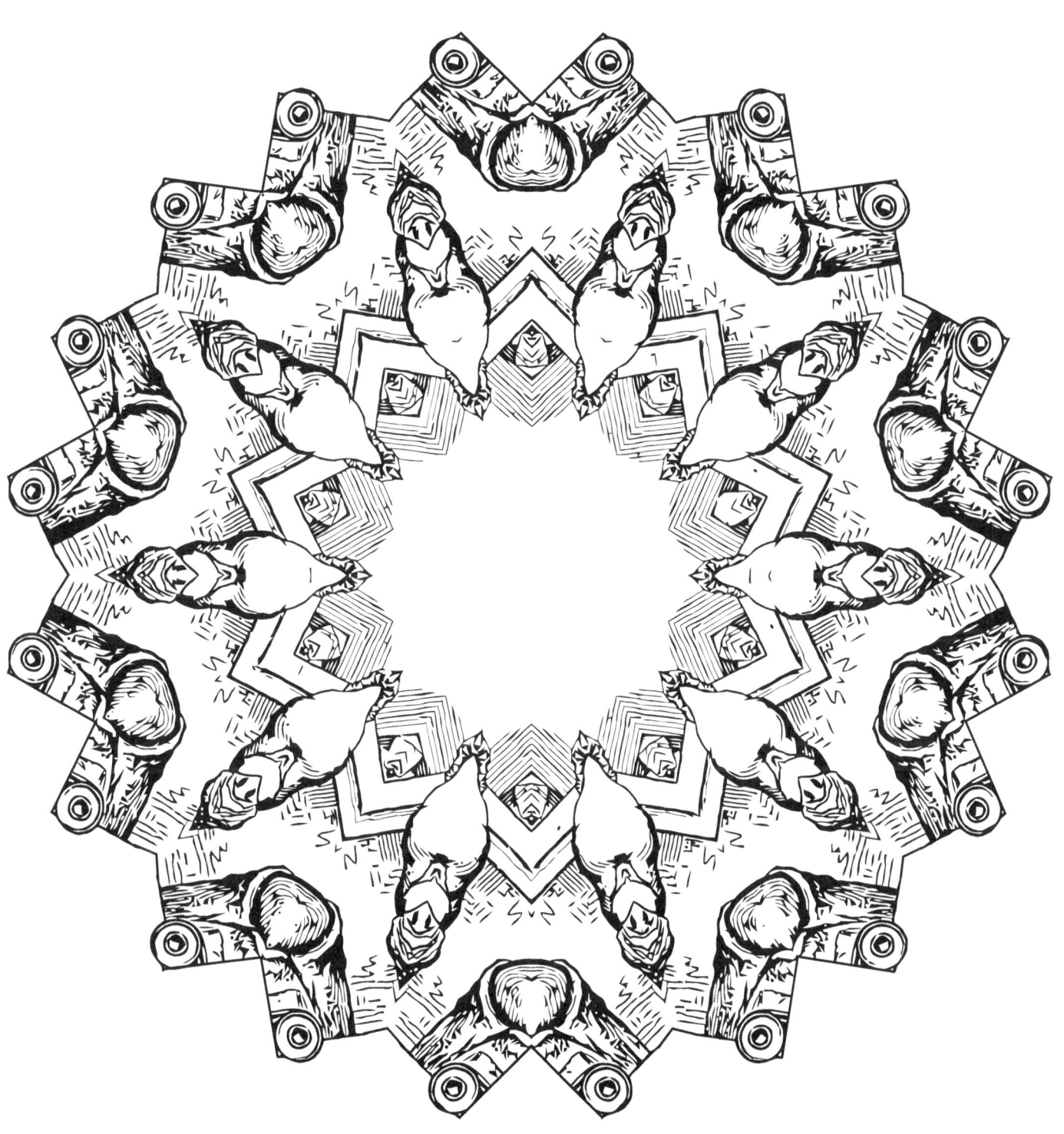

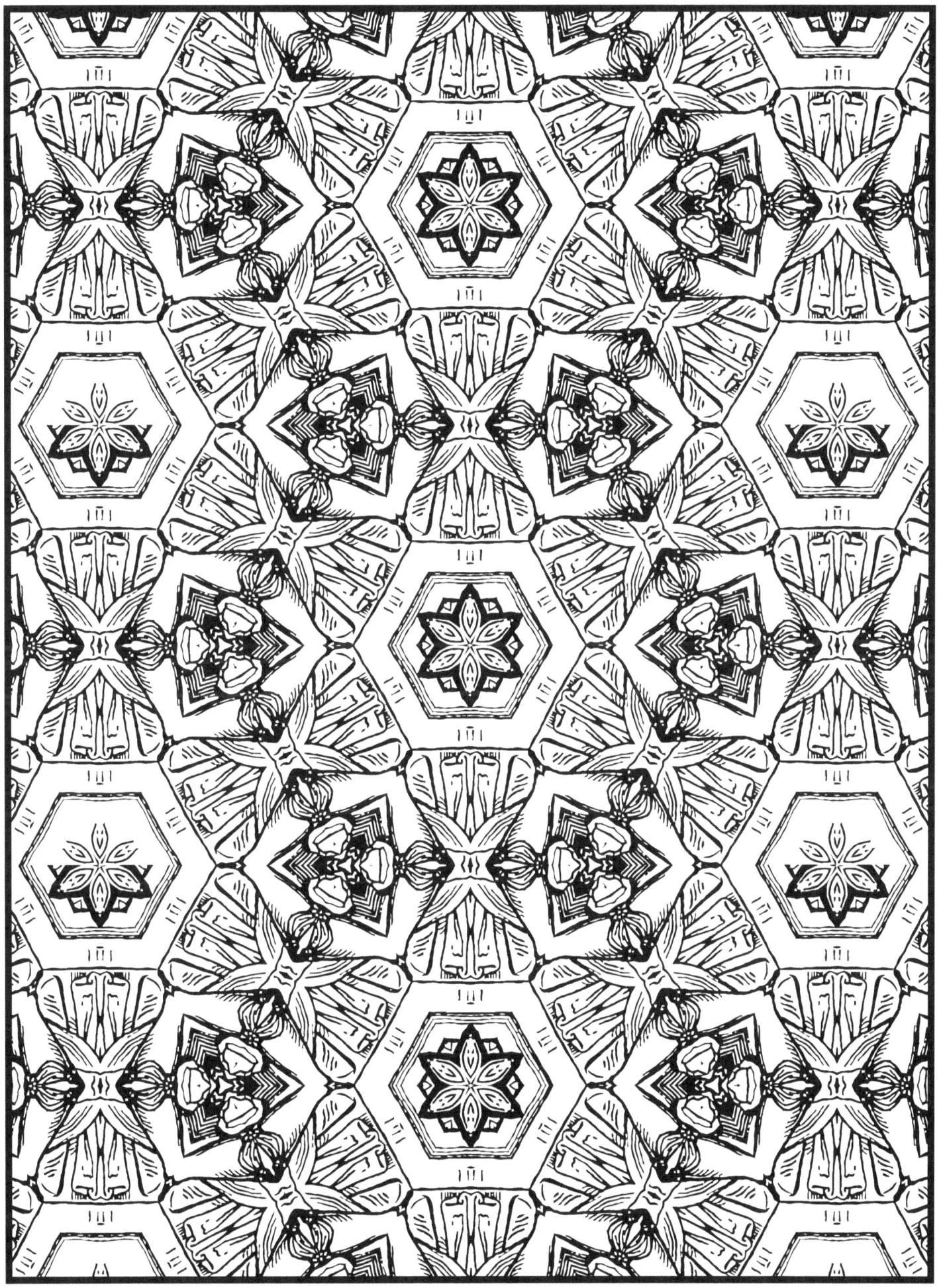

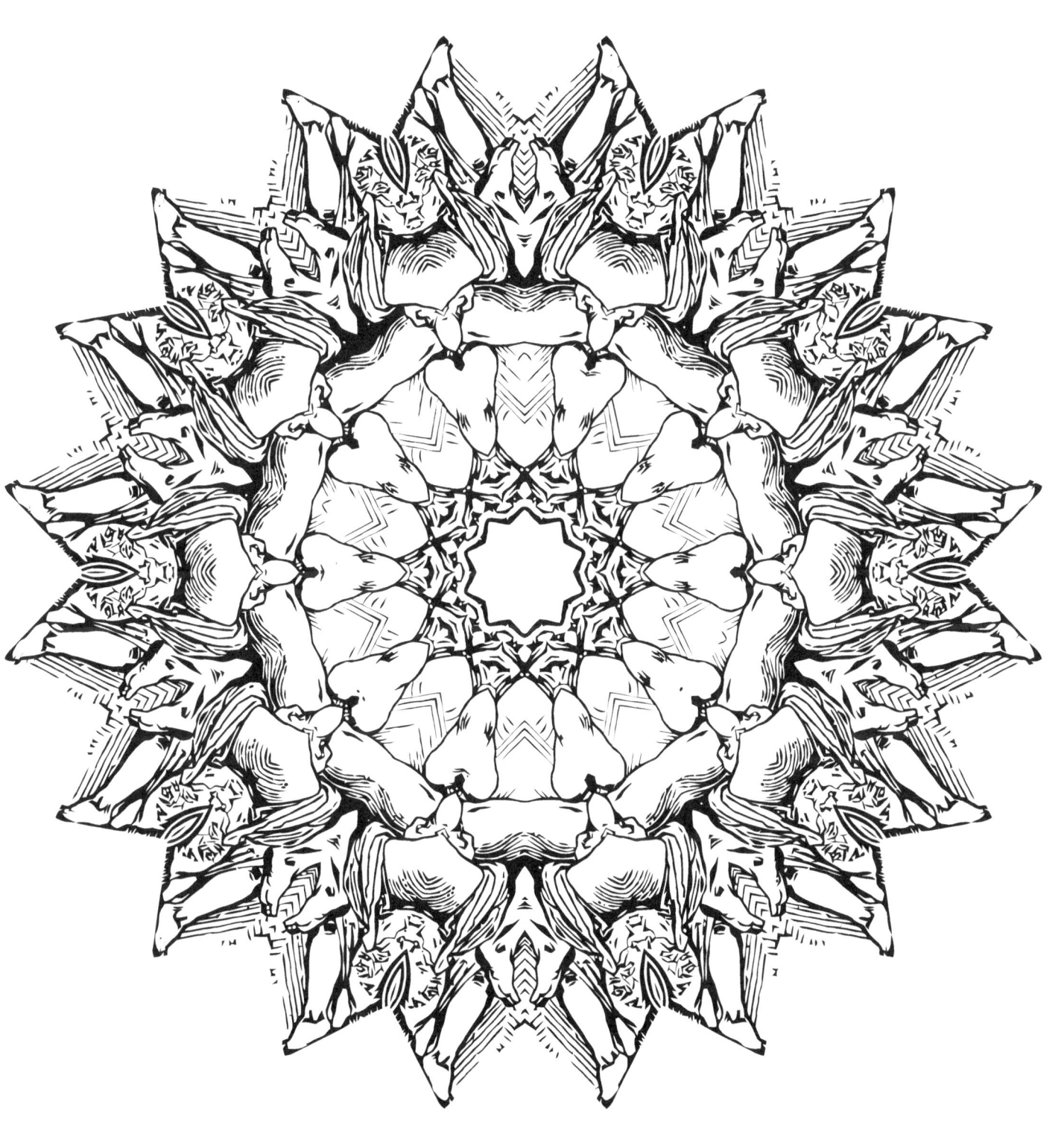

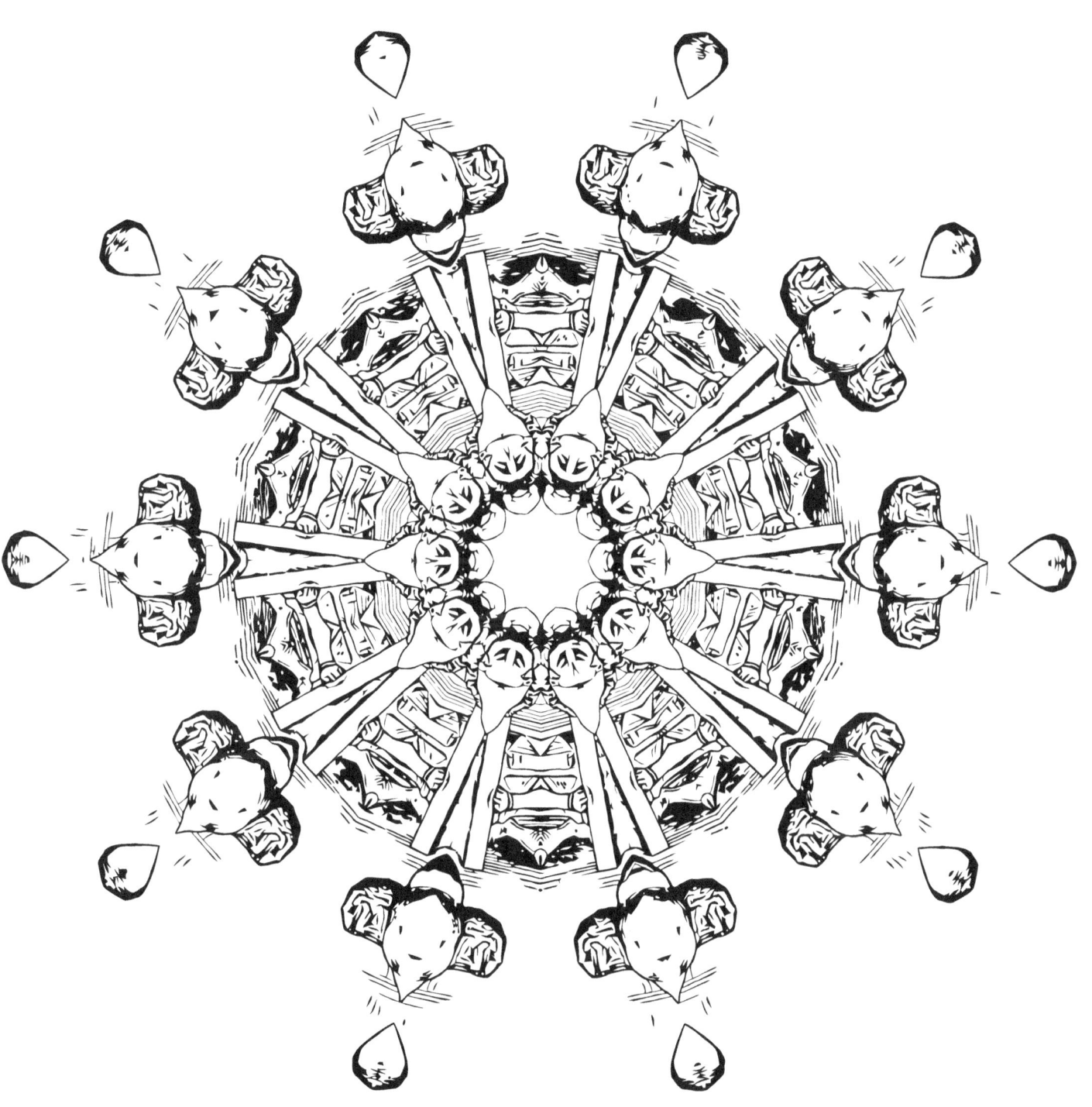

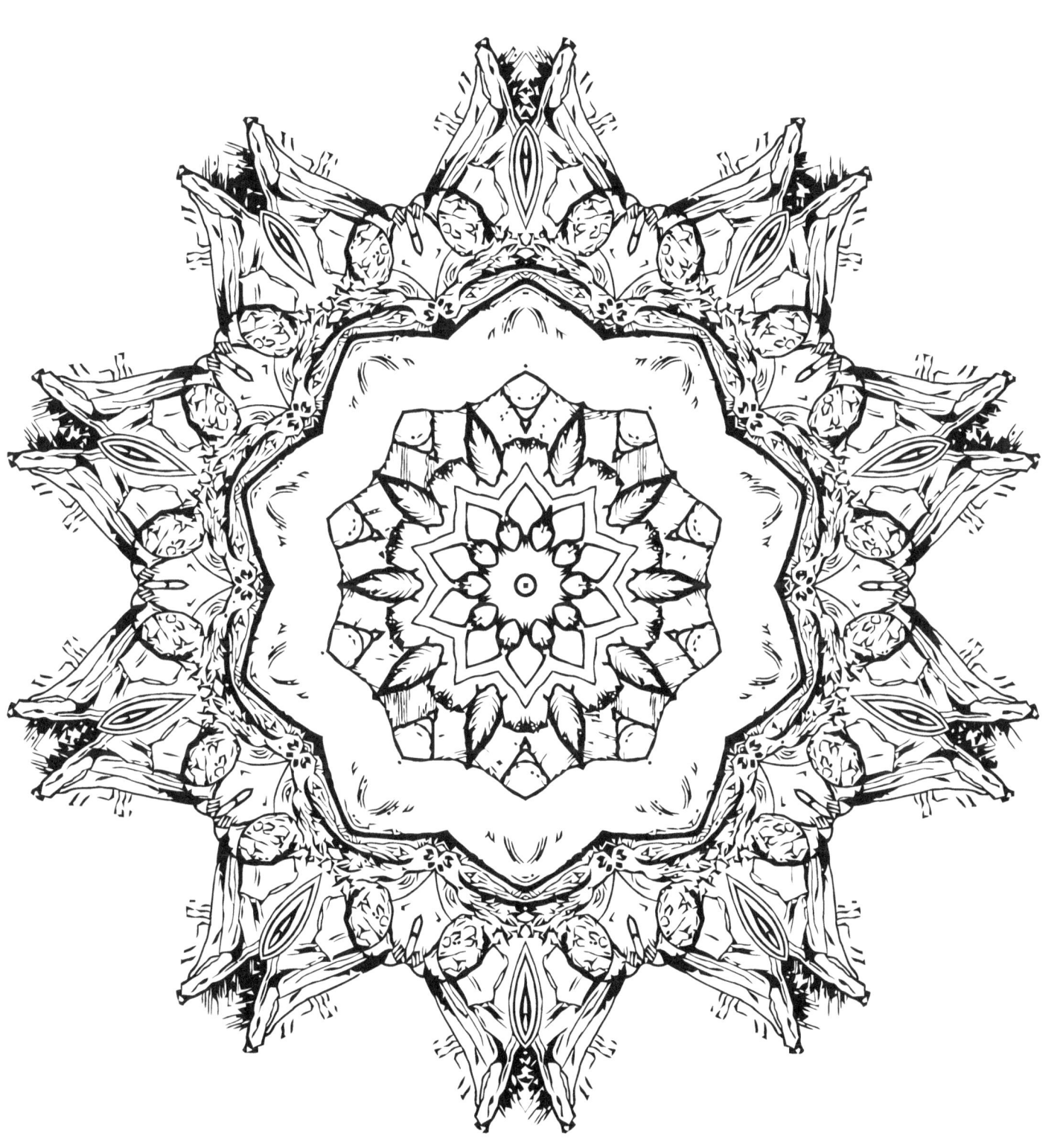

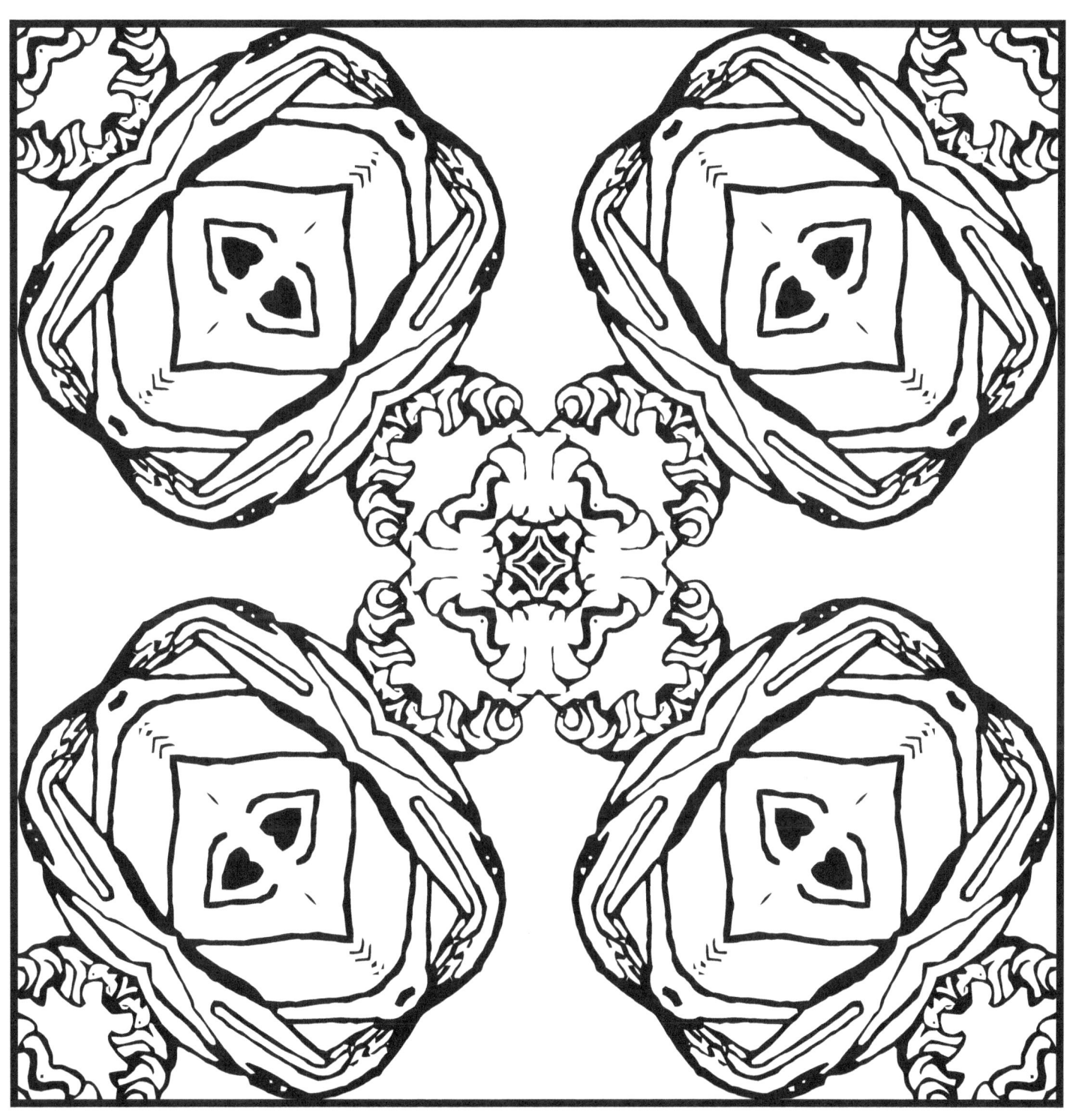

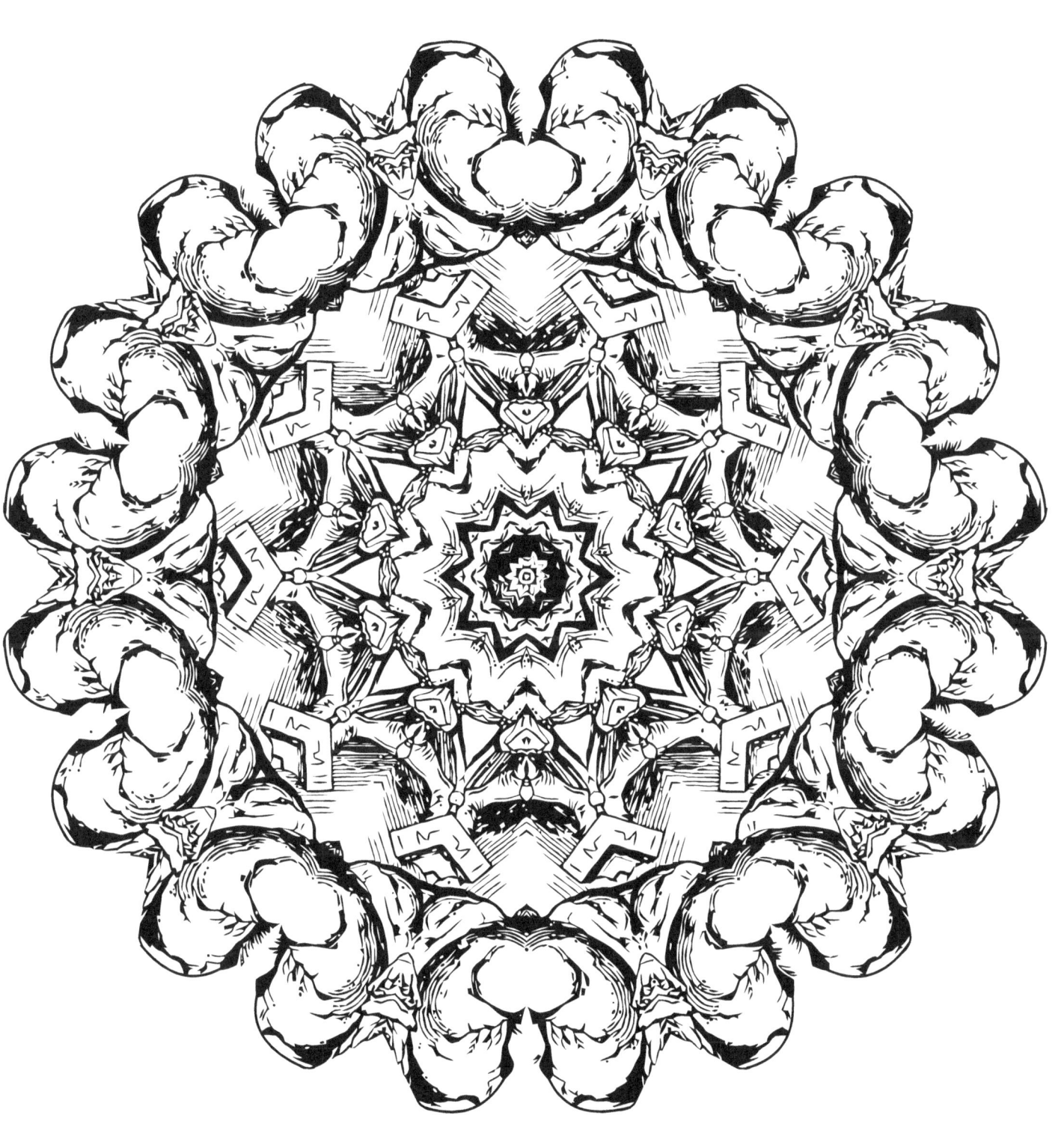

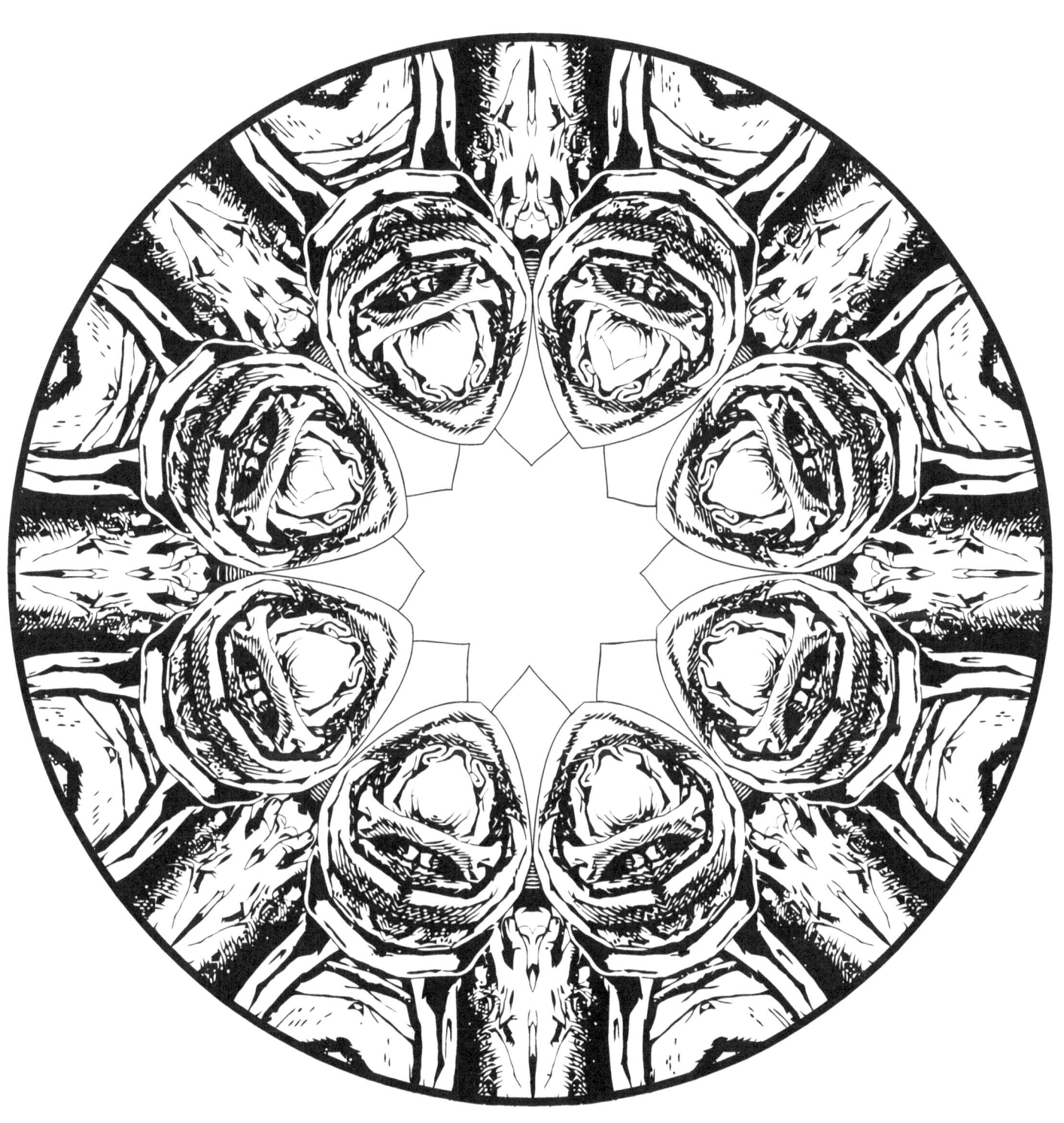

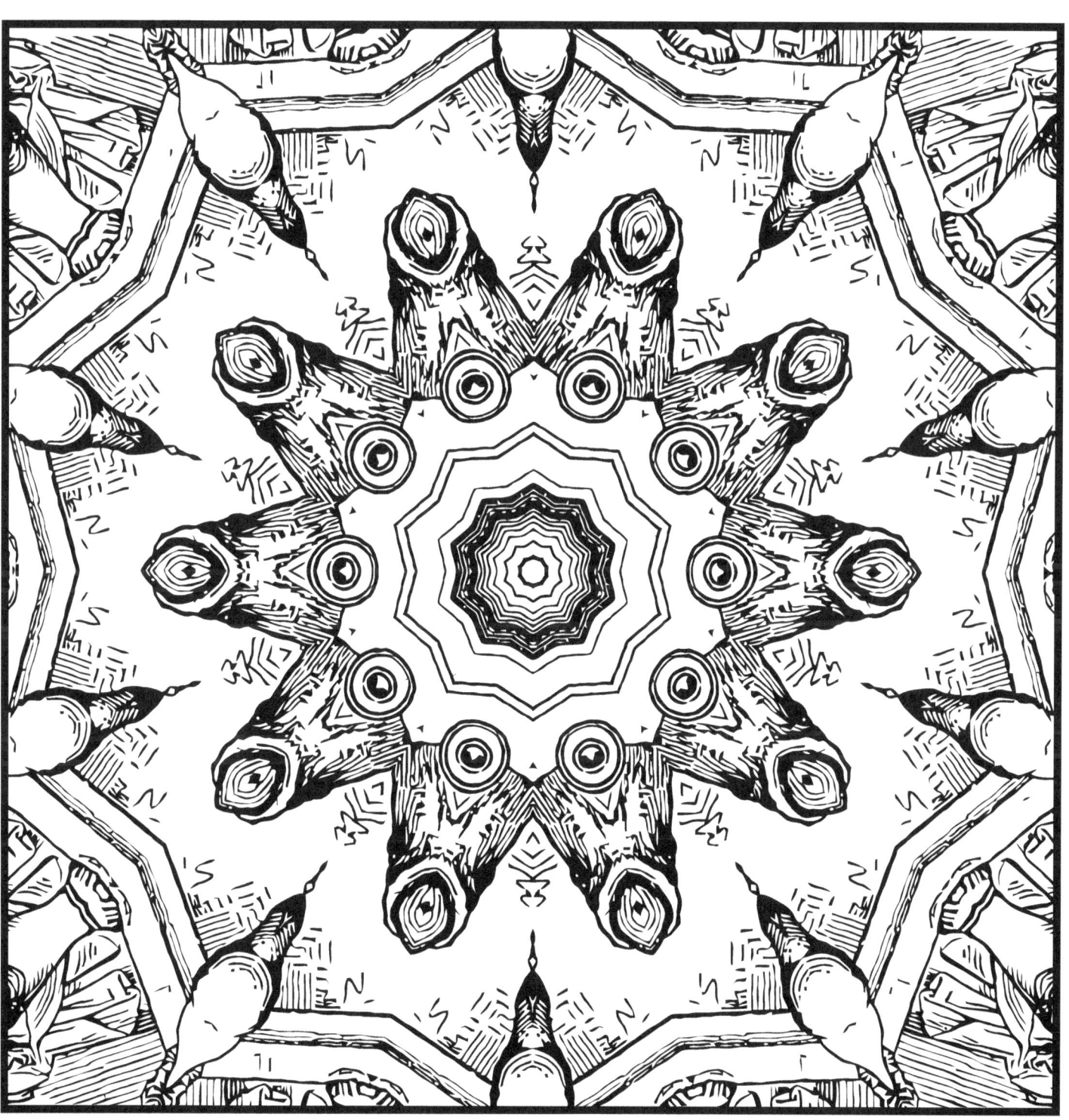

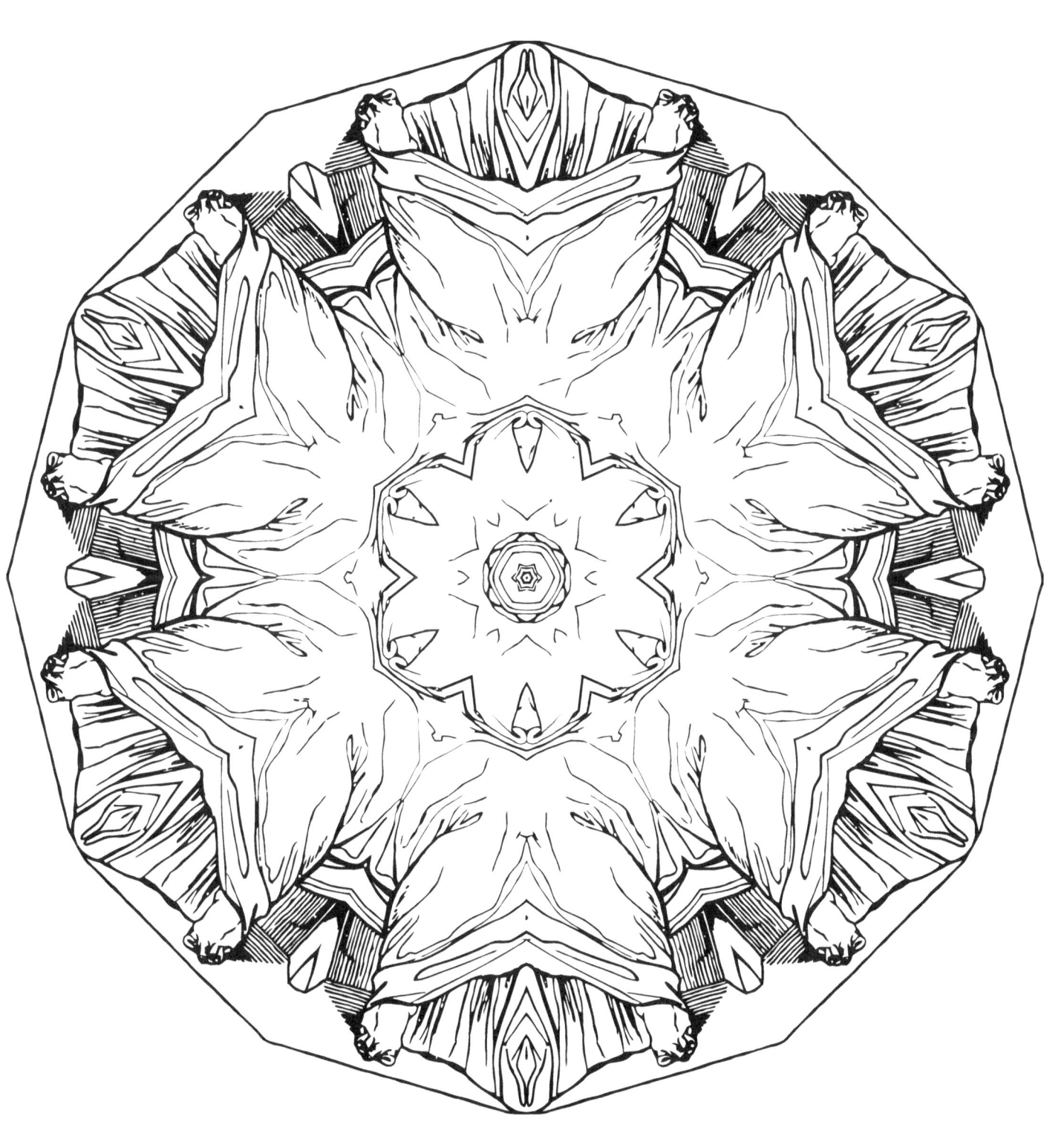

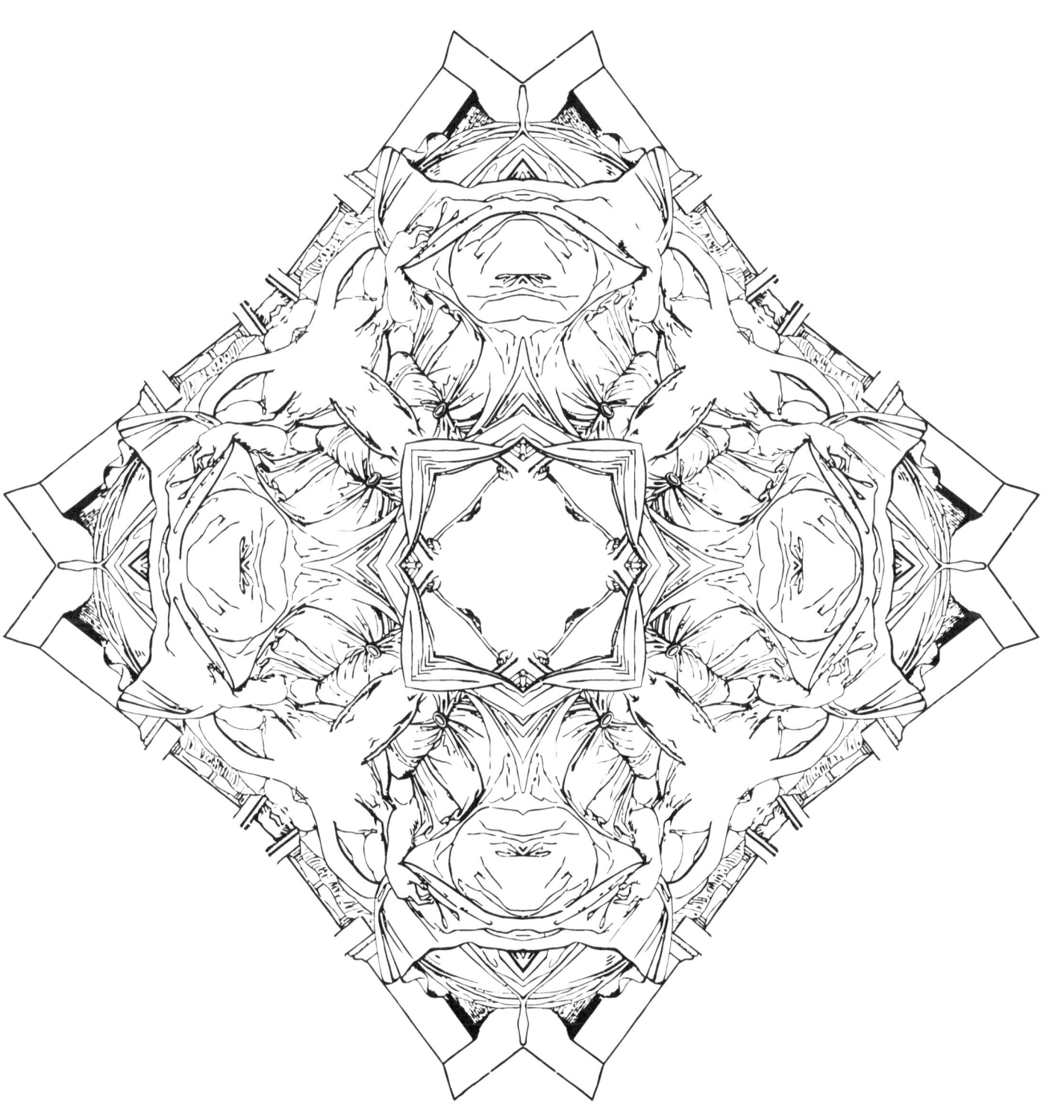

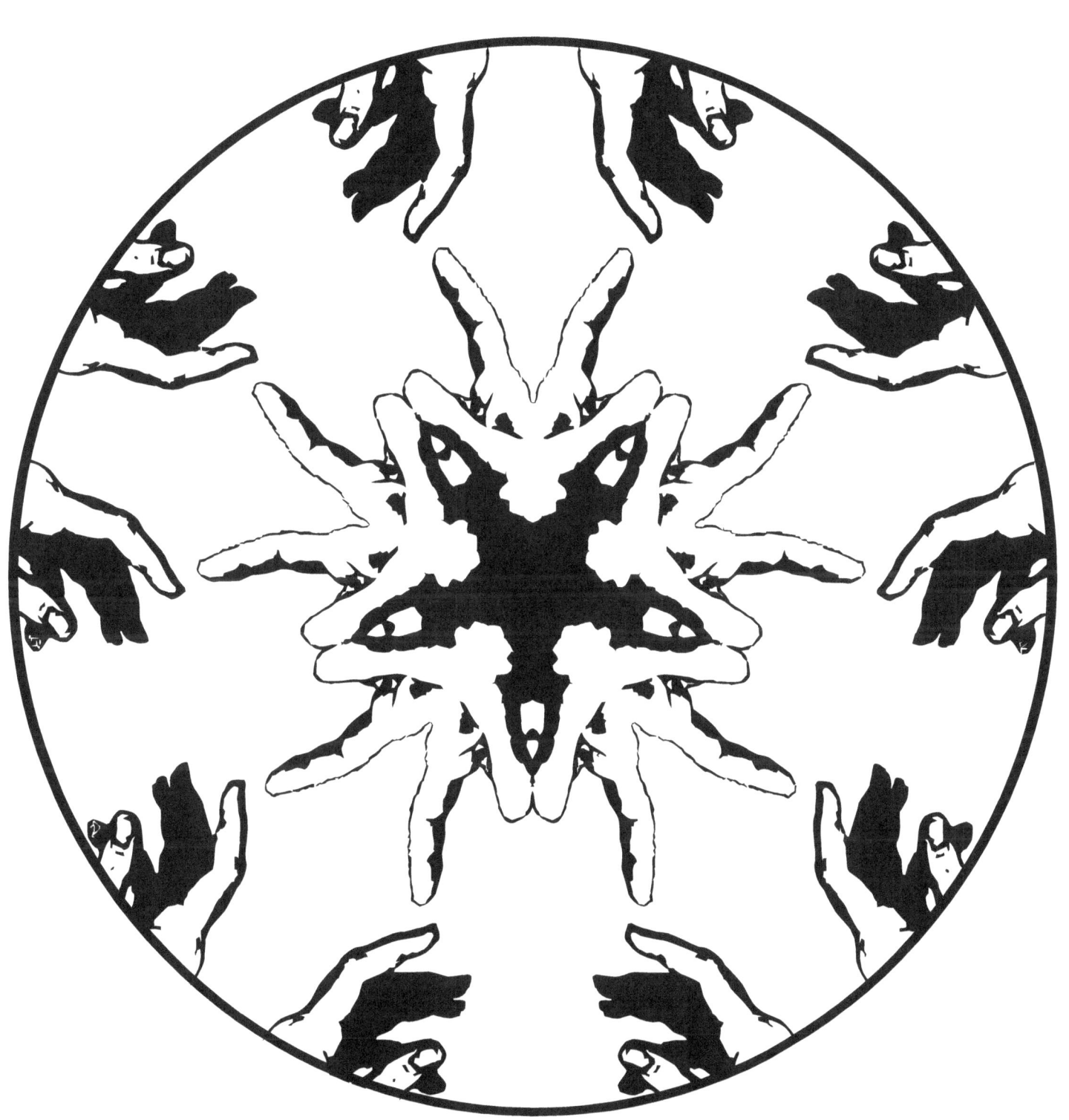

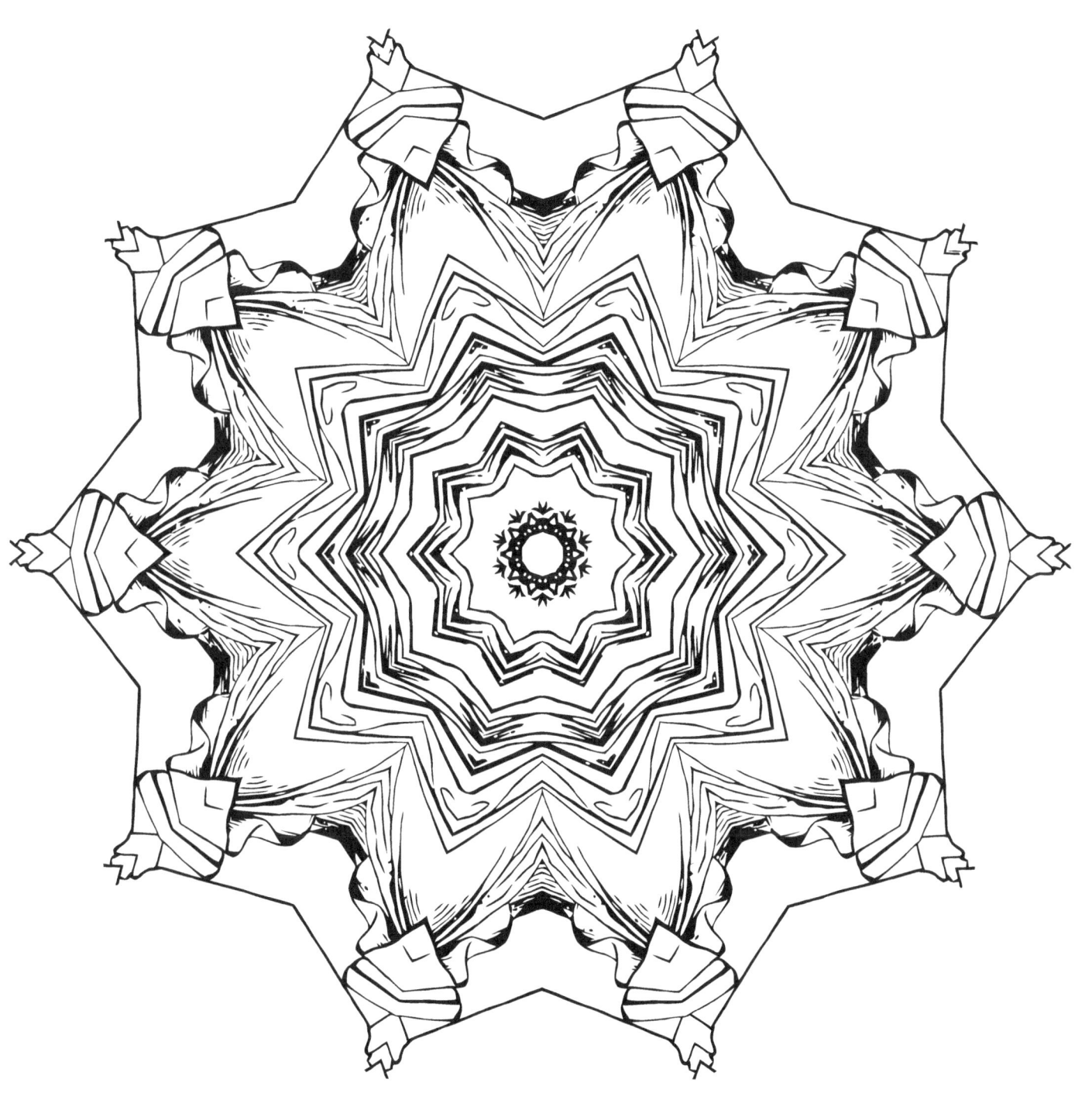

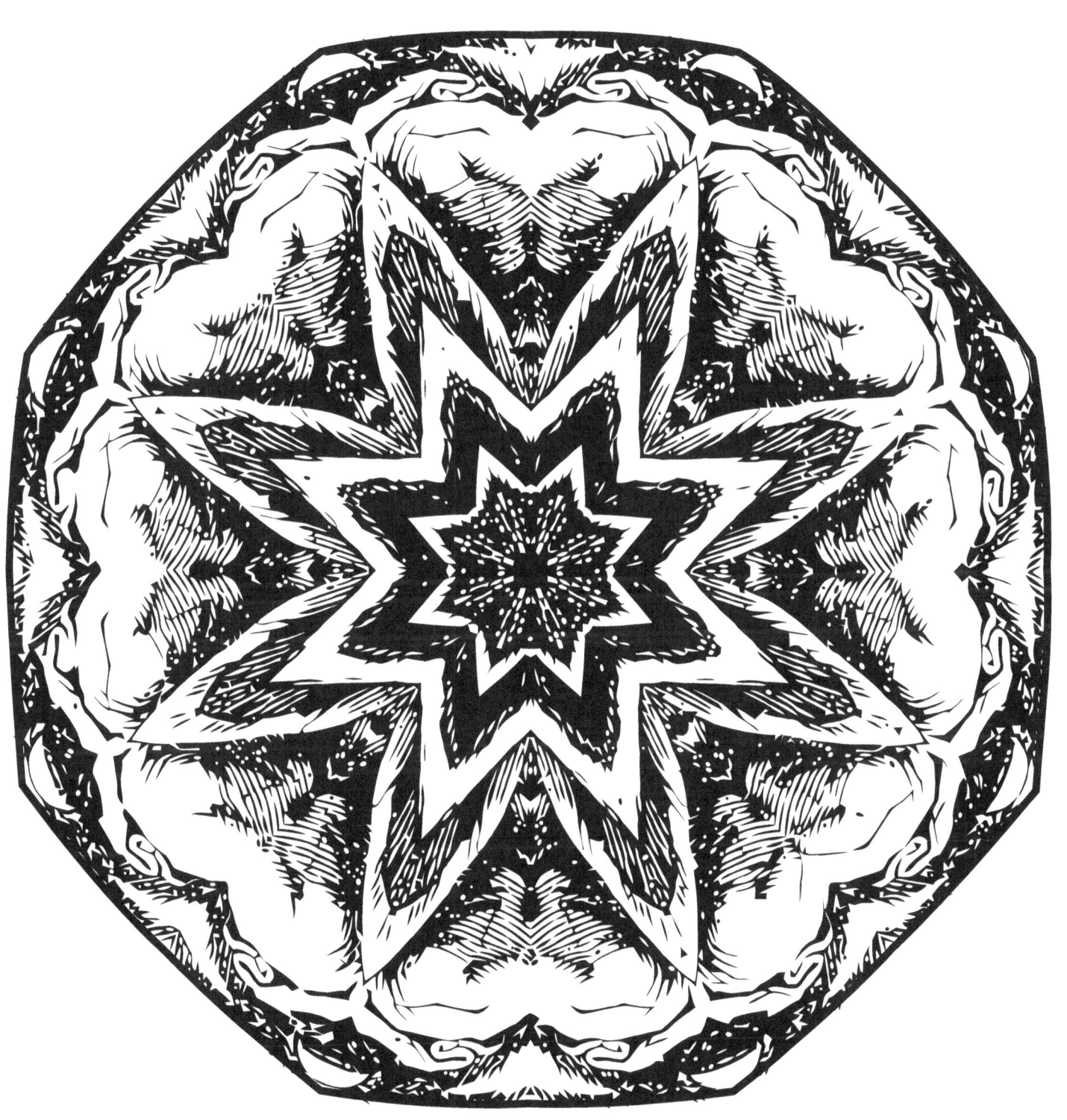

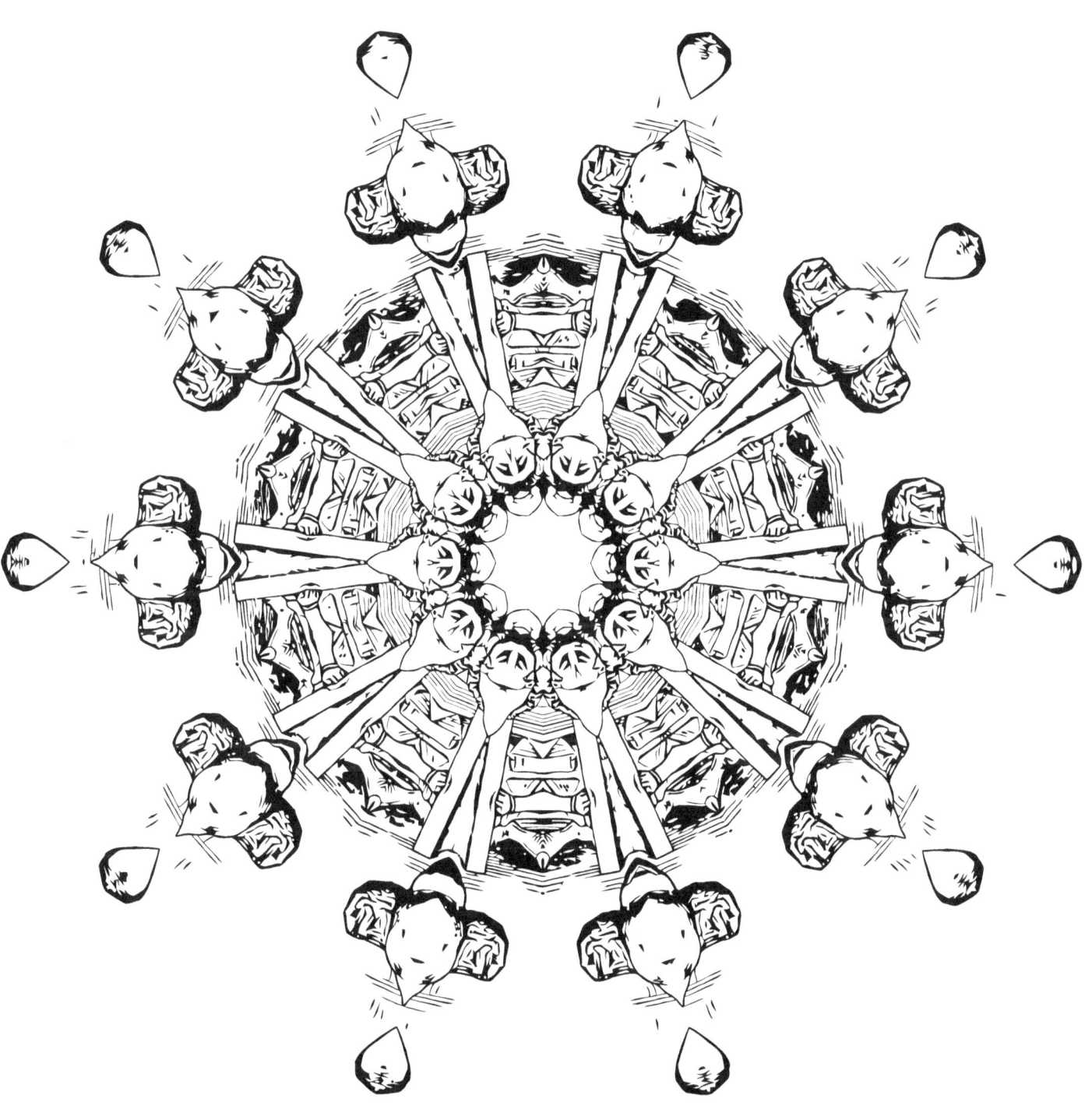

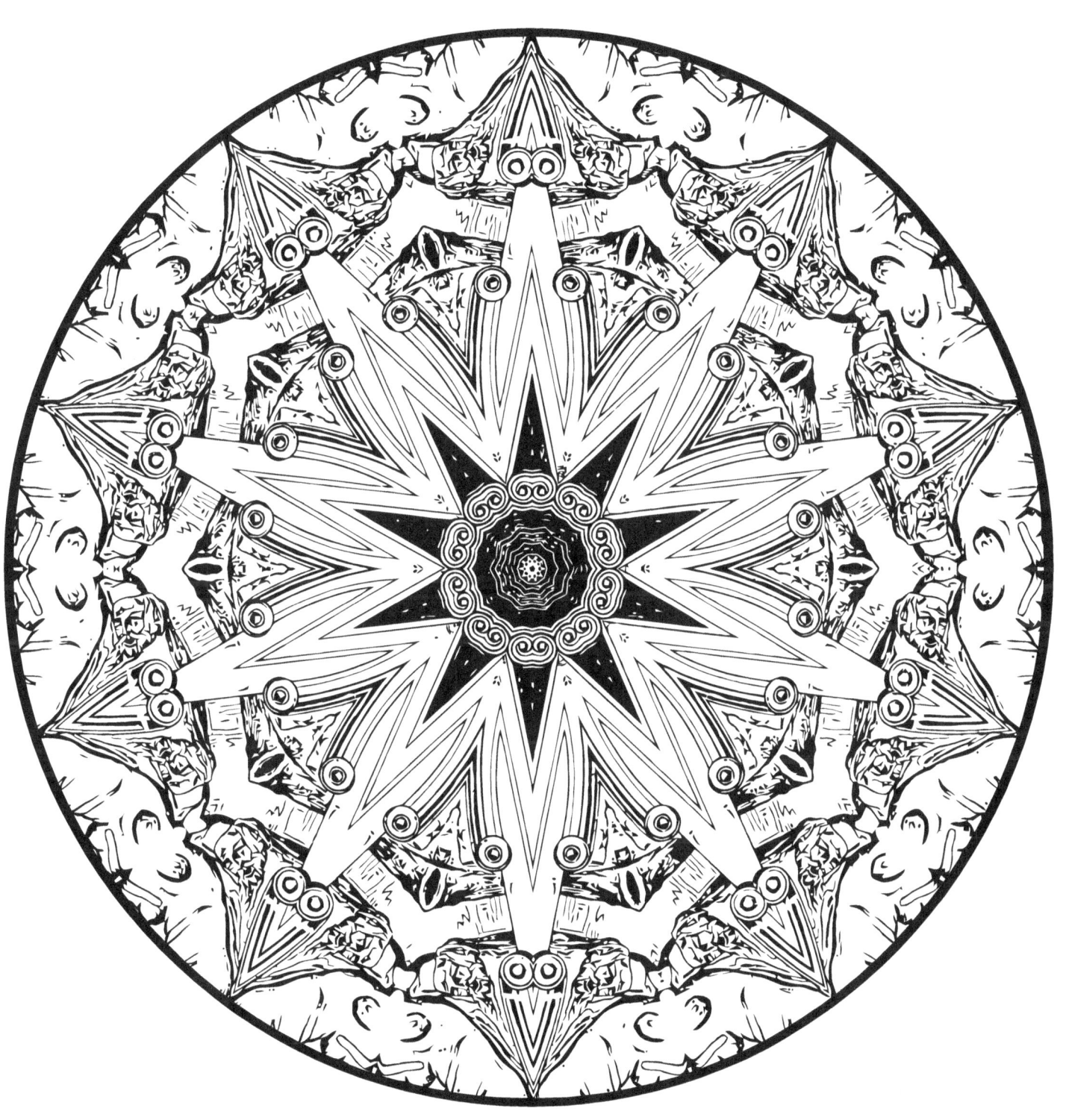

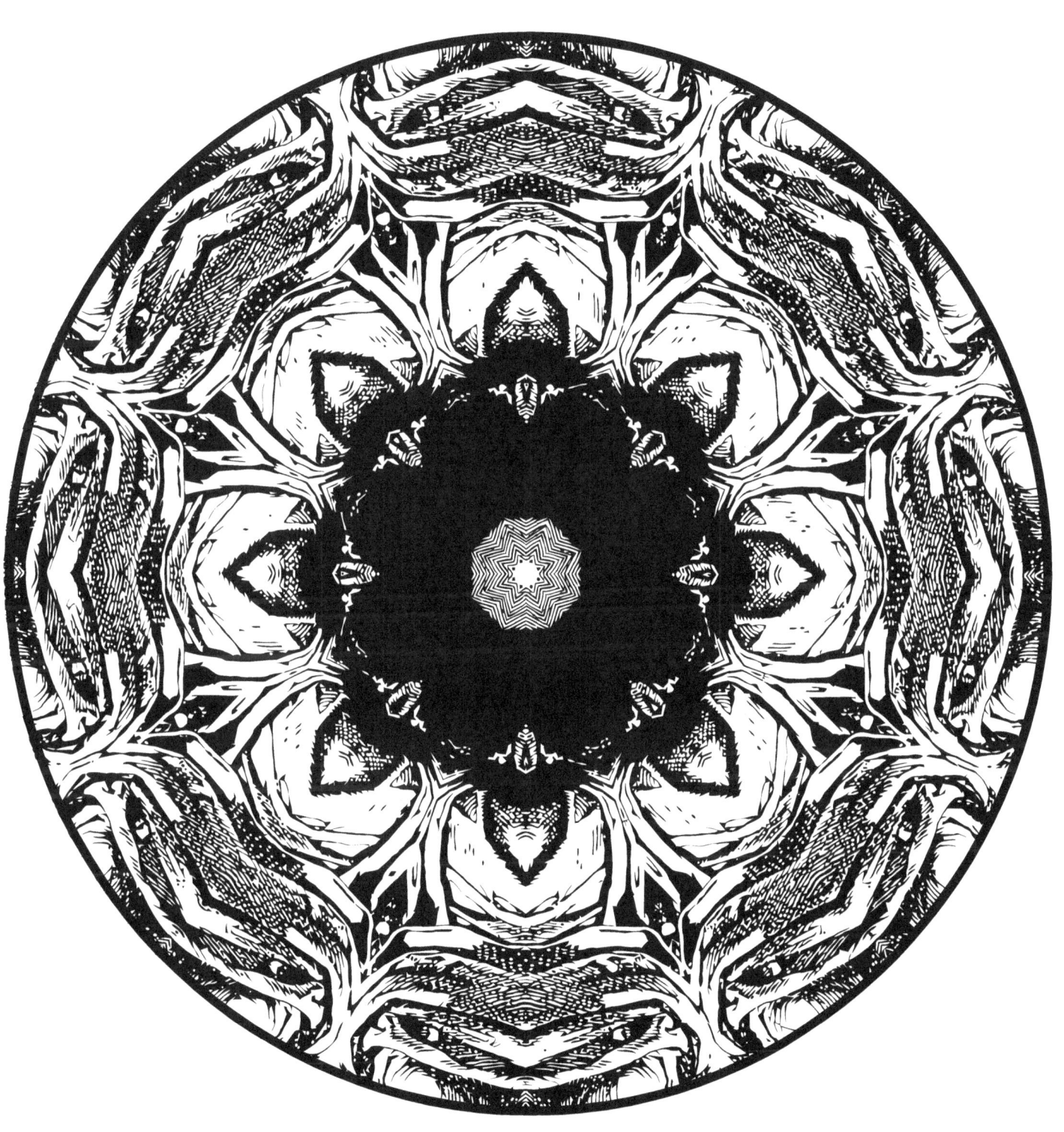

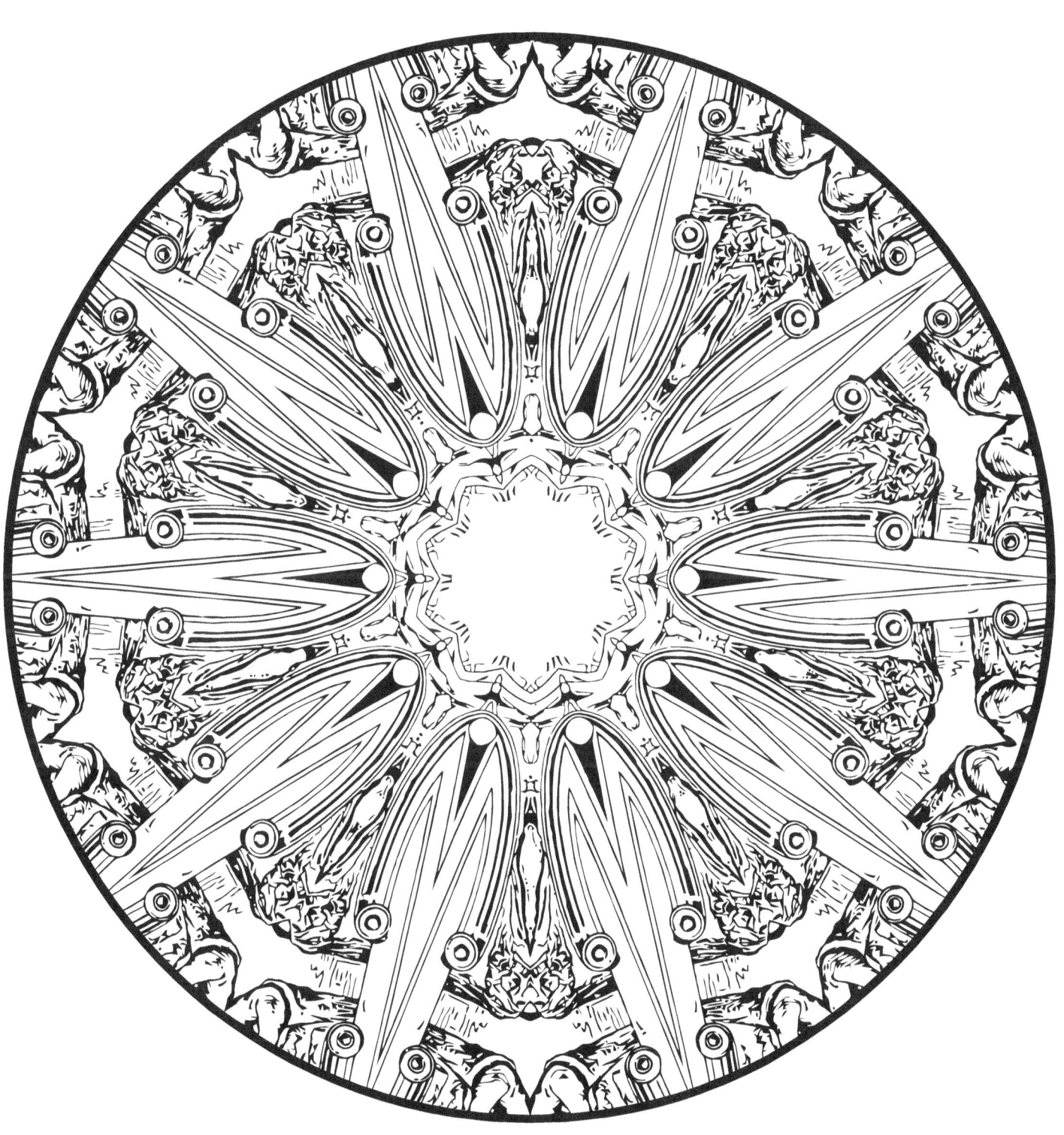

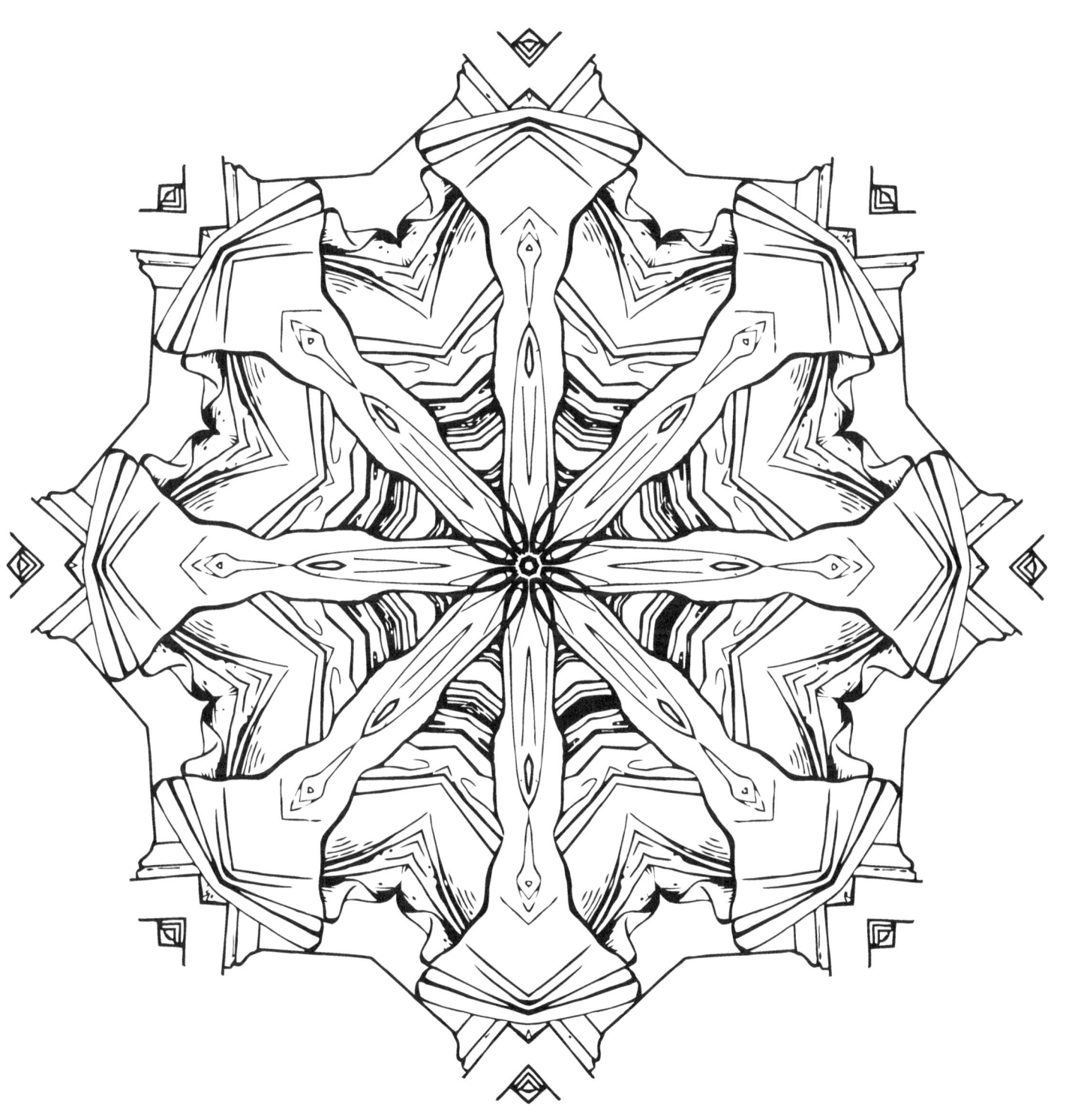

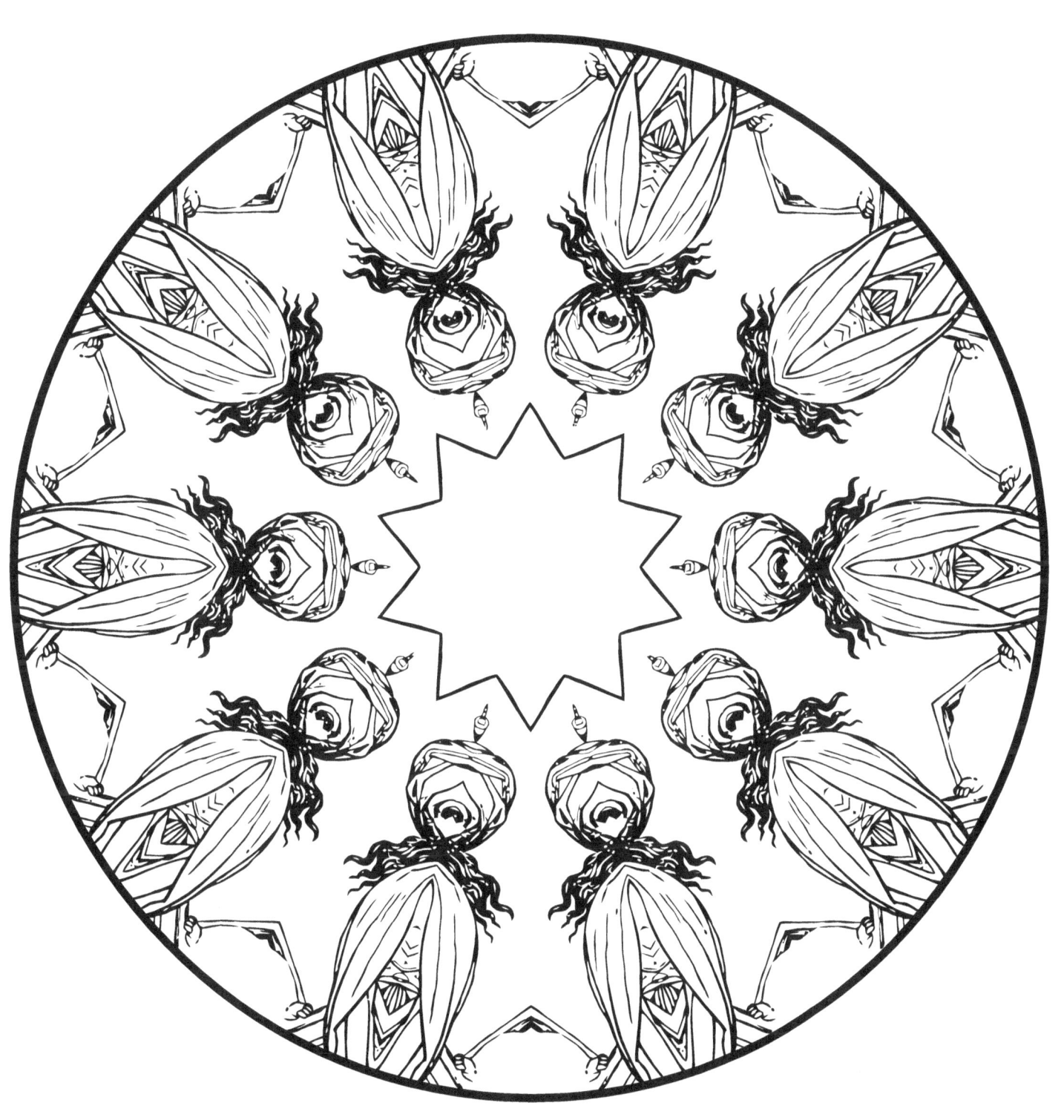

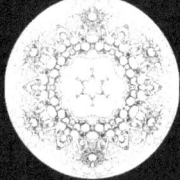
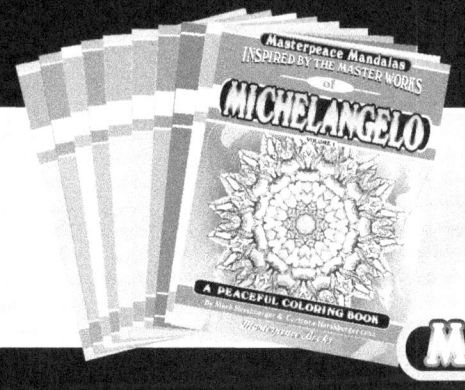

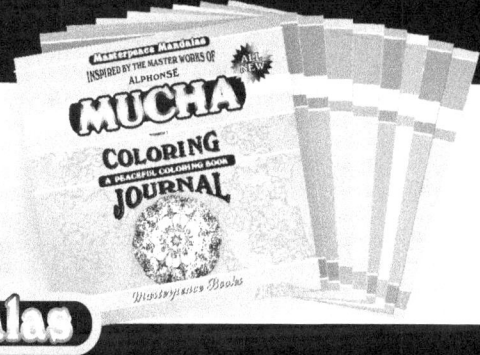
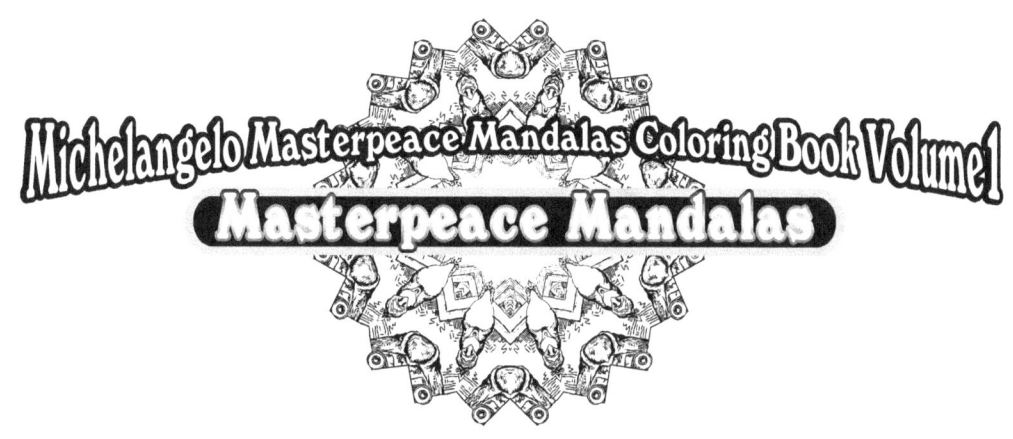

Michelangelo Masterpeace Mandalas Coloring Book Volume 1
Masterpeace Mandalas

Tip - Carefully Remove This Page And Place It Under The Page Your Working On To Protect The Next Page

www.ingramcontent.com/pod-product-compliance
Lightning Source LLC
Chambersburg PA
CBHW081733220526
45468CB00008B/2088